Surface
TENSION

Love, Sex, and Politics
Between Lesbians
and Straight Women

Edited by Meg Daly

A TOUCHSTONE BOOK
Published by Simon & Schuster
New York London Toronto
Sydney Tokyo Singapore

TOUCHSTONE
Rockefeller Center
1230 Avenue of the Americas
New York, NY 10020

TOUCHSTONE and colophon are registered trademarks
of Simon & Schuster Inc.

Designed by Deirdre C. Amthor

Manufactured in the United States of America

1   3   5   7   9   10   8   6   4   2

Permissions acknowledgments begin on page 253.

Library of Congress Cataloging-in-Publication Data

Surface tension : love, sex, and politics between lesbians and straight
women / edited by Meg Daly.
p.   cm.
"A Touchstone book."
1. Lesbians—Biography. 2. Heterosexual women—Biography. 3. Bisexual
women—Biography. 4. Friendship—Case studies. 5. Lesbianism.
6. Feminism. 7. Bisexuality. I. Daly, Meg.
HQ75.3/S87   1996
305.48'9664'0922—dc20   95-34619   CIP
ISBN 0-684-80221-X

Acknowledgments

First, thank you to all the contributors for their work and words and thanks to the many women who sent in prospective pieces. This book is for all of you. I'd like to thank Anna Bondoc for the initial inspiration and encouragement and for her continued friendship. And thank you to the many people who gave me suggestions, shared lists of writers, and in some way facilitated the making of this book, especially Cathy McKinley, Sarah Schulman, Jackie Woodson, Sarah Pettit, Karen Auerbach, Ira Silverberg, Malaga Baldi, Steven Friedman, Gail Motyka, and Kit Robinson.

Thank you to my family and to my friends, especially Joanne Pendola, Michele Huyette, Ericka McConnell, Claudia Gorelick, Jeff Hoffman, Lisa Mediodia, and Jen Stein for their feedback and support throughout all phases of putting this book together.

Thanks to my agent, Charlotte Sheedy, and to Aviva Goode for her tireless commitment to this book. And thanks to my editor, Cindy Gitter, for her belief in this project, and to her assistant, Andrew Stuart.

For Shannon

Contents

Introduction

With all the recent hype about "lesbian chic," and with half of the *Village Voice* women-to-women personals signed by "bi-curious" females, it's clear that the line between lesbian and heterosexual women is becoming murky. Suddenly it's hip to think, talk, look like, and even be lesbian. Beyond the media's romance with lesbians, however, exists the very real fact that straight women harbor an intense curiosity about what it means to be a dyke. Many straight women are intrigued and inspired by the thought of living unbound to male fantasies—unbound to male anything—in a realm in which a woman can just be a woman.

Furthermore, behind the media's discovery of lesbians lies a long, rich history of daring dykes working in the struggle for social justice, making art, or just living their lives. These women have worked in league with heterosexual women in their communities and, in many cases, have formed strong, long-lasting bonds of friendship. In more recent history, these bonds have been explored in writings such as the interview reprinted here of feminists Robin Morgan and Gloria Steinem. Dorothy Allison also lends a historical perspective to straight-lesbian relations in the 1970s in her piece entitled "Conceptual Lesbianism."

Many of the stories and essays in this anthology take the form of personal narrative, exploring a particular friendship or perspective on relationships between women of different sexualities. My own deepest friendship with a straight woman began in third grade, well before I came out as a lesbian. Shannon and I met one day on the playground and almost instantly formed that unparalleled bond of "best friends." We spent countless hours together involved in elaborate rituals of play. We created skits, watched *Fantasy Island* religiously, danced madly to the Bee Gees in our living rooms, set off on wild adventures in the woods of Wyoming, and dreamed of someday living in the world described in *The Clan of the Cave Bear.*

As Shannon and I matured, there were periods of distance. We became involved in school activities and began dating boys. But we maintained a secret and otherworldly bond that we both trusted was forever. We ended up going to the same college and lived together for two years. I remember one bike ride we took near a rhododendron garden in southeast Portland, where we planned our future together after college. We were to live in a big house and run a bookstore-café. We would have children together, and the men in our lives would be secondary. We would constitute the nucleus of a family. We referred to ourselves—and still do—as soul sisters.

I came out the year after I graduated from college. By then Shannon had fallen deeply in love with a man who has now been her partner for four years. When I reflect upon my relationship with Shannon, I see that it was my primary love relationship for many years. Within our "best friendship" were the seeds of what would grow to be my desire to love women, to form primary bonds—emotional, physical, spiritual—with women.

In her essay, "Between Girls," Lisa Springer reflects on the period in her adolescence when she didn't have an awareness of attraction between women. She wonders how having this awareness, then acting on it with her best friend, would have changed the nature of their friendship. The desire for people of the same sex remains unarticulated and unrecognized longer in some women than in others. With the choice to articulate your sexual orientation come the problems of when and how to do so and, occasionally, the wish that you didn't have to. In Guinevere Turner's narrative "Kat," Guin recounts an unexpected meeting with a childhood friend in a bar where the friend, Kat, is tending bar. When Kat asks Guin about her role in the lesbian film *Go Fish,* Guin is gripped by a momentary hatred toward the dykes who accompanied her to the bar, "because I feel exposed by them."

As in the case of Shannon and me and of Guin and Kat, many lesbians and straight women are able to grow beyond their differences and may find themselves appreciating certain nuances of their relationship even more. There is inherently a lesbian nature to my friendship with Shannon. There is a romantic and erotic quality to the energy and love we share, although it's not fully enacted. Would these qualities be recognized if Shannon and I both identified as straight women?

When I asked novelist Jessica Hagedorn if she had experienced attraction between herself and other straight friends, she answered yes, but went on to say that "there is more permission to explore this feeling with lesbian friends." She goes on to express her dissatisfaction with labels of any sort. She, a Filipina woman, is often expected to claim an allegiance to one "camp" over another—Asian-American, woman, artist, feminist. She finds these labels extremely limiting, including labels concerning sexual orientation. Is it a form of heterosexual privilege for a straight woman not to have to claim a sexual orientation? Conversely, is it a way of staying in the closet for a woman who sleeps with women to refuse to claim a lesbian identity? The truth is, identity politics rarely coincide with the complexities of the lives we live. We love and feel attraction to many different people in many different ways.

The way we experience sexuality is also informed by our racial and ethnic background and customs. In Martha Southgate's story, "The Kick Inside," the reader is left feeling unsure about what will happen between the straight black narrator and her white lesbian friend. We learn that the narrator, Pam, has had to cross both racial and sexual boundaries to trust her new friend. The attraction she feels for Rebecca is acute, jolting, transformative. I don't read this piece as a coming-out story—too many questions are left unanswered. I read it quite literally as the story of one woman's world being rocked and torn open by another woman who is very different from herself.

The first time I ever fantasized about having sex with a woman was during my sophomore year in college. Maria was a lesbian, an African-American, a musician who more than stood out on our mostly white, pseudo-progressive liberal arts campus. She was known to lift her shirt while walking to class, revealing her bare breasts, and pronounce, "If men can do it, why can't we?" I'd reserved a little corner of my mind for her, into which I would crawl, late at night, and imagine kissing her, our bodies pressed together. To me, coming from a conservative white rural background, she was everything I wanted to be: brave, irreverent, sexy, independent. Four years passed before I would actually say to myself, "I am a lesbian." When I came out, I was saying to the world not only that I wanted to have sex and primary relationships with women but also that I aspired to be a certain kind of woman, the kind of independent woman I had lusted after, someone who spoke her mind and did not live by society's rules.

• • •

While compiling this anthology, I spent many hours on the telephone and at cafés, hearing contributors' stories, getting the stories behind the stories, laughing, and comparing notes. I talked to straight women who did not know any lesbians and to lesbians who had no heterosexual women friends. I also spoke with lesbians whose best friends were all straight women and with straight women who wished they were lesbians. Some contributors ultimately withdrew their submissions, finding it too painful or complicated to publish accounts of their close friendships. I want to thank the many women who in some way, through writing and conversation, put their energy into making this anthology happen. The essays and stories collected here expose truths and intricacies within women's friendships and familial relationships. The contributors, some emerging writers, some well-known and established writers, have written beyond boundaries of sexual orientation to further our understanding of women's intimate bonds.

Meg Daly

New York

1

Best Friends

Between Girls

by Lisa Springer

In high school in Iran I was in love with my best friend, Miriam. We had a passionate emotional closeness, and I remember moments with her in minute detail; the feel of the physical world around us remains clearer to me than anything surrounding me in the present. But she wasn't a lesbian, and at the time I didn't know I was. Now, with the knowledge of who I am, I can go back to those sharp memories and make sense of the emotional confusion that colored our interactions, and I can understand the detours our relationship took—like the time I had an affair with her father.

Our dynamic, a battle for domination, began the day Miriam and I met. She was twelve and I thirteen when she transferred to the French school I was attending. On a clear September day, beneath the particularly bright blue sky of high altitude, we stood in the courtyard of the school, lined up to walk past the woman who would inspect our uniforms. Miriam stood very straight, wearing a red skirt that peeked out beneath her immaculately ironed blue smock. I asked about her life, and she answered in English with the British accent she had acquired at her last school.

I learned that her parents, an Iranian father and a French mother, wanted her to work on her French now that she had perfected her English. She lived in the northern part of the city, up a steep hill, in a house with a big yard and several dogs. In the afternoons, she was very busy with piano and Farsi lessons, but after she finished her studies, she was allowed to go horseback riding. On weekends she liked to ski, and the summers, of course, she spent at the seaside in France.

I felt poor and scruffy in comparison. My parents were both American, which seemed much less exotic to me. Both from immigrant families—one Irish and one German—they were proud of my father's steady ascent to the position of midlevel officer in the Foreign Service. I lived with them and my five brothers and sisters in a small house that we were told we were fortunate to have. That morning my mother had dug my smock out of a box, and it was wrinkled and smelled like old clothes. I was wearing yellow plaid pants that were too short and revealed my white socks. After school, if I was lucky, I would play Monopoly with my siblings. I had never had a private lesson in anything.

I found Miriam beautiful. Her straight dark brown hair had the weight of a cascade of water rushing down a mountain. It glistened in the sun, and I considered touching it to see if it felt like silk. Her eyes, set close together, made her seem vulnerable, while her rigid back made her seem unapproachable, even snobbish.

I walked over to my friend Yasmine and kissed her on both cheeks. "Plaid pants that are a bit short are the rage in the United States," I told her. I didn't look back to see if Miriam was watching me.

Yasmine, as always, was wearing her smock open, revealing a black miniskirt underneath. She and I were planning a little rebellion against the school rule that we had to keep our smocks closed. We would convince our classmates to cut off all the buttons on their uniform by the next morning. While I thought about Miriam's perfectly pressed clothes, Yasmine and I walked up and down the row of students telling our friends that the uniform infantilized us and we needed to take charge of our own destinies.

I ignored Miriam for a good half hour. Then I turned to her. "Welcome to the school," I said, as an afterthought, as if I didn't care. I explained that she should cut the buttons off her uniform that night.

"My mother wouldn't want me to do that," she said.

I laughed. "I wouldn't let my mother run *my* life," I said, knowing as I said it that this was an easy way to put her down.

Our rebellion failed, so Yasmine and I began smoking cigarettes in the bathroom. Meanwhile Miriam sat in the front of the class, and I watched her from the back row. The barrettes in her hair changed frequently. I memorized the stiffness of her shoulders. She invited me to her house on the hill to play on her trampoline in the afternoons, after her lessons. And one afternoon she told me about the plum trees in the garden in her family's house on an island in France, and the jam they made from them.

"We eat it with fromage blanc. You'll love it."

This is how I learned that I would go with her to France. For years it surprised me that Miriam invited me anywhere, even though she did so regularly. I had the total self-absorption of a person in love. I thought about Miriam all the time, but I never wondered about her feelings. I thought about the way she finished a plate of fromage blanc and plum jam, bringing the plate up to her mouth and licking it. I remembered her telling me that hands symbolized a person's being better than any other part of the body. But I never wondered what it was like to be her or how she might feel about me. I never thought that she liked me and that I could hurt her, too.

One afternoon during that first summer at the house on the island in France, Miriam felt sad and wanted to stay at

home reading and listening to music. She assumed I would
do whatever she did. She informed me that we wouldn't be
going out that day. I felt trapped inside the house, trapped on
her turf. Miriam didn't say that she needed me, and I didn't
say that I was waiting for her to tell me she did. I told her I
had other plans, and she attacked.

"I invited you because my parents think that vacations are
more fun for me if I have a friend."

The rounded wood door, set into a stone wall at the end of
the garden, stood open. I held my bicycle—Miriam's from
the previous year—away from me, ready to jump on. "I am
not your paid companion," I said.

"My father is making this trip possible for you," Miriam
said.

"I'm going to play with Caroline," I replied.

"She's my friend," Miriam said.

"And now she's mine."

I bicycled down the little alley that led to the center of
town. Vines with delicate flowers peeped through stone
walls. My wheels crunched small pebbles and my heart
pounded.

"I am not Miriam's possession," I told myself. "I am not
the friend of the year, like the bicycle of the year, the new
model."

Caroline's house lay beyond the square at the center of
town, behind a church. From a balcony off her bedroom, we
could see the tiled sloping roofs of the houses in the center
of town. We sang American songs. Caroline told me she was
really happy that I was there for the summer. When Caroline
said this, I thought about Miriam for the first time that afternoon. I decided that Caroline probably liked me better than
she did Miriam.

Now, twenty years later, I wonder how Miriam felt, spending the afternoon alone. Her friend listened to her closely
and then disappeared when she most needed her. Her friend
admired her but surrounded herself with other people, even
when she stayed at Miriam's own house. She acted as if she

were at a hotel, coming and going as she pleased. I'm sure that at that moment Miriam vowed to invite a different friend the following year.

But as the summer approached the next year, Miriam began sharing her dreams of being back in France. She talked about the plum jam and fromage blanc. This time, I too had memories that added details to the idea of summer on the island. I remembered watching Miriam's eyes as she licked her plate clean. They crossed just a little at the same time that they lost their focus. She seemed completely involved in what she was doing. I tried licking my own plate but found that it was not as satisfying as it looked when Miriam did it. She also talked about riding our bikes in the salt marshes. "We should do more athletic stuff this summer," she said. I noticed the word *we* and didn't even wonder whether I would accept her unspoken invitation. Miriam never formally invited me, and I never stated that I would come. We fell back into my being part of her vision of the summer.

Miriam found my independence a challenge. We continued to dance around each other's desires, my running away a surefire way of confirming that I could affect her, even if I believed it only during the moment of her anger. And so, year after year, I watched her dark body become tan, and I told her as we sat on the beach that her knees were fine.

"They're too thick for my body, fat even," she said.

"They're glorious," I said.

"You're lying," she said.

"Okay," I admitted, although I had been telling the truth. Her knees separated her well-defined solid thighs from her much finer calves. This seemed perfect to me, a combination of strength and delicacy in each leg, the knees incidental in themselves but beautiful as part of the whole.

I tried to explain something of this to her. "If you look at any one part of a body closely, really closely, separate from the others, especially a joint, it's bound to be ugly."

When Miriam stood on the beach and shook her hair out behind her, I was reminded of the beautiful power of a horse.

She held her head high and moved her limbs in the wind, as if getting ready to unleash the energy held inside her body. Beneath her small firm breasts, her stomach was completely flat, descending sharply, like the sheer drop of a cliff to the ocean. Her legs with their thick knees seemed like the perfect base for this sculpture. I didn't think Miriam had a complaint.

She must not have believed me, because we had this conversation again and again, the summers blending into one another, our sentences one year merely variations on those of the previous year. One year she brushed my hair for a long, long time.

"I feel so insecure," she said. "I have so many complexes."

I didn't answer and I didn't move. I believed that I had a monopoly on insecurity and so I didn't need to say anything to console Miriam. I didn't move because I wanted her to continue to touch my hair, and I feared that a motion on my part might give her the idea of stopping. If I stayed in the exact same position, I would will her to do the same, to brush my hair forever.

I kept my head tilted forward and looked at the couch cushion, white with a burgundy flower sewn on. My neck hurt after a while, and I wondered how we would make the transition from touching to not touching. But although I sat rigid the whole time she had her hand on my head, inside my body my nerves were jumping around frenetically, anything but still, dancing and playing as if nothing else in the world mattered.

Interestingly, it was she who initiated our most physical and intimate moments. I thought too much about brushing her hair to actually be able to do it. And one afternoon I thought about kissing her stomach.

We were playing at her house in Tehran when Miriam told me she wanted to take me to a secret place. We walked through the trees to the back of the garden, Miriam leading me by the hand. We came to a clearing. To my great surprise, Miriam unbuttoned her jeans and lay down on the ground, face down. She wiggled her body like a snake, pushing herself up against the dirt and the grass.

"I love the earth," she said. "And when I put my naked body up against it, I feel close."

I stood watching Miriam, wondering why it had never occurred to me to put my stomach up against the earth. I wished I were Miriam because I wanted to be spontaneous and sensual and free. I imagined myself undressing and rolling my body in the sand at the beach. I would do this—another day. On this day, desire was imprisoned inside my body. I wanted to reach out and touch Miriam, but instead I reached up and moved a curl away from my forehead. I wanted to lie down in the grass next to her, but my legs felt like tree trunks that had roots in this spot. I hated my immobility.

When Miriam rose, her face was flushed. *Beautiful,* I thought. I looked at the blades of grass that had molded themselves into the flesh around her belly button. That's when I thought about kissing her stomach, placing my lips against it and pressing them into her flesh.

Instead, I kissed her boyfriend. Miriam went to the mountains for a weekend with her father. The excuse was that he had just bought a new sports car and wanted to try it out. I always felt envious of their closeness and shut out from the oddly romantic aspects of their relationship. That weekend, at a party, when Miriam's boyfriend followed me into an empty dark room and began to kiss me, I didn't push him away.

It didn't take long for Miriam to find out what had happened. On a bus going up to the ski resort two hours north of Tehran, she told me she knew I had made out with her boyfriend.

"He told me the two of you kissed for over an hour," Miriam said. "He removed your bra from beneath your pink sweater and played with your breasts."

I looked out the window at the treeless mountains covered with blinding snow. Miriam's bluntness shocked me. I really didn't want to hear the whole scene described. I had been there and wanted to forget about it.

"He said that he was aroused because, after all, he's a boy and you're a girl and you were lying on a bed together touching one another, but he doesn't feel that you're very passionate."

I listened, feeling that I had little choice. After all, I was the one who had committed the sin, and I was thankful that Miriam was speaking to me at all.

She continued. "You kiss in a tentative way, and your breasts are very white and soft. He took off his shirt, but you didn't touch his chest. He said you seemed afraid of it."

I looked for a break in the monotony of the landscape but saw white in all directions. I wanted to tell Miriam that she shouldn't go out with that boy. He kissed roughly and had been most pleased when I was awkward. He loved conquering and humiliating his partner. Besides, he was hairy and too strong and insensitive and boring and self-involved.

I knew I had little right to criticize him. But I thought about the hairs that peeked out of his nostrils and the leer on his face, and I convinced myself that I had to speak up. "He's always unfaithful to you," I said softly, looking down at my lap.

"At least he's honest," Miriam said. "That's more than I can say for you."

Miriam and I skied separately that day but rode home together, exhausted, sleeping on each other's shoulders. Half asleep, the bus jolting us through darkness, I felt the sharp pain of contrition. I deeply regretted spending those two unpleasant hours with her boyfriend. I vowed to be a better, more loyal, and more understanding friend.

I believe that I sincerely intended this. But the intensity of my response to Miriam twisted my feelings into a multitude of desires. I wanted to have her, to be her, to hurt her. And it was often when I hurt her that I came closest to having her.

One summer Miriam's father planned a party at the house on the island that included his friends as well as Miriam's. Late at night he and I danced together, close. I saw Miriam walking around the room picking up empty glasses while I felt her father's hands slide up and down my back. She sat in a chair and watched us for a few minutes before she came up to us and pushed us away from each other.

"Come out to the garden," she said to me.

In the garden she did all the talking. My head was spinning from drink as I heard her say that we had gone too far and that I had no respect for anything, including her feelings. I felt deeply ashamed of myself but exhilarated to know that she cared.

During my first year in college, I received a telegram from Miriam's father inviting me to go with him to the Bahamas or Las Vegas, whichever I preferred. Standing in front of hundreds of gray mailboxes on the first floor of my dorm, I read the line, "The beach or gambling?" and I remembered Miriam's reproaches. I immediately sent my answer, "The Bahamas." I had a fantasy that Miriam would be on the trip with us, reprimanding us. I had seen pictures from trips that Miriam had taken with her father to exotic places. The two of them in a pink Jeep, the two of them with snakes. I imagined that I could jump into the picture too, no longer just the friend that Miriam invited along, no longer a second-class citizen. I could become a real member of the family, another daughter with whom the father was in love, Miriam's sister.

Her father and I sat beneath a palm tree sipping drinks with multicolored umbrellas in them. Behind us, in a cage, a parrot repeated the five words of its vocabulary. We had just had sex, and I felt confused and sad and didn't understand why.

"How do you think you would feel if Miriam were in this same position?" I asked, trying to make sense of my own feelings. "For example, if she were having an affair with my father?"

Miriam's father leaned back in his chair and laughed. It was the laugh of a man at a poker game whose adversary has told a joke, a staged laugh accompanied by a hand slap on the table and a thrown-back head. And then he stopped as suddenly as he had begun.

"She wouldn't be," he said coldly.

Of course not. Miriam never took more than tiny steps

away from her own family. When we lived together in Tehran, she didn't like to spend the night at my house. She needed to take care of her dogs, and she didn't want to leave her mother. I invited her to the Caspian Sea with my family for a four-day weekend in a cottage at a middle-class resort, but she decided to spend the time with a new horse at the stables. She had a completely full life with school and lessons and vacations, parents and a boyfriend and me, her best friend. Miriam didn't have the constant longing that consumed me during my adolescence. I looked and looked for something I could not find.

In my mind I tore up the picture I had created of Miriam and me with her father in a pink Jeep with snakes around our necks. I decided that I didn't want to stay in the Bahamas for the full five days we had planned. We left the palm trees and the parrot and spent the rest of the day at travel agencies finding a flight back to New York.

As we were about to land at Kennedy, Miriam's father had an idea. "We could have a quickie in the bathroom at the airport." He looked at his watch. "I have three hours before my flight for Paris takes off. It wouldn't even have to be so quick."

"No, thanks," I said.

I wanted something. I could taste it in the extra saliva in my mouth. I could see it in the brightness that my desire cast on the colors around me. I didn't want to have furtive sex with Miriam's father in a public bathroom at Kennedy Airport. Still, I wanted something.

I took a taxi back to my dorm with the twenty dollars Miriam's father gave me. I watched the lights of the city moving past me and tried to find the right cool, distant tone in which to inform my friends, "It was hot in the Bahamas, and I couldn't focus on my reading of Marx." In truth, I was ashamed of having run away from Miriam's father. I wanted to be more mature, able to have wild affairs without emotion. I thought this was the solution to my confusion and yearning.

What would have happened if I had known that I wanted to make love with Miriam? I had all the evidence I needed, but I was missing one vital clue: the awareness of attraction between women, between girls. I can't really know what the gift of information would have done for my life. Perhaps I would now be writing my memories of a first sweet romance with Miriam. Perhaps not. Still, whatever the shape of my life, looking back, I wish I had known what was going on. Understanding would have opened up choices.

I didn't see Miriam for a year after the trip to the Bahamas. On the first night of my arrival at the house in France, I told her about college, about the way American universities work, and about the men I had slept with. Always more graphic than I, she brought up the question of circumcised versus uncircumcised penises. She wondered how a woman's pleasure was affected.

"I've never noticed the difference," I said.

"Even with Papa?" she asked.

I felt humiliated and tricked. We had been speaking for several hours in a friendly way, and all the while she had known that I betrayed her. I had been boasting of my experience, portraying myself as a woman of the world. "I've had sex with five men," I had said. The words came back to me, sounding superficial, mocking me. Miriam had set the whole thing up, organizing the conversation so that it would lead to her query: "Even with Papa?"

"He's not circumcised, you know," Miriam said.

Actually I didn't know, and this added to my humiliation. I was a liar and a fraud. Neither a good friend nor a woman of the world. Having allowed me to pretend to be both, Miriam sat tall in her chair and looked at me without pity.

"You've had sex with at least one uncircumcised man," she said. "Surely you can say something about the difference."

I felt stuck in the particular space I occupied in the air, as if my silhouette had been cut out and placed there. I couldn't move or say anything.

"Or you could say something about the experience. Just about the experience with Papa."

I looked down at the thick dark wood of the table. I thought about the many hours that Miriam and I had spent at this very table over the years, talking and talking, trying to figure out the world and ourselves.

I had missed her enormously during that year. Being in the same room with her, I remembered her smell, especially strong at the point where her neck joined her shoulders. I remembered that she loved the sand and the ocean water and rabbit with mustard sauce.

Eventually, Miriam spoke. "I've known you for many years," she said. "And never in all that time have you been at a loss for words."

I looked up and saw that she was smiling. I didn't dare return the smile.

"I'm glad to know I have power over you," Miriam said.

I smiled then. This was as close as Miriam would come to admitting that I mattered to her.

"You must be tired from your trip," she said. "It's time to go to bed. Tomorrow we'll go sailing."

I wanted to stay up all night listening to our favorite Neil Young album from the previous year. When the sky turned light, we could go to the bakery and get a fresh loaf of hot bread, bring it back to the room at the end of the yard where I always slept, and eat it with butter and strawberry jam. Then we could go to the beach and sleep all day in the warm sun, waking up every once in a while to run into the ocean.

"You're right," I said. "It's late."

I kissed Miriam on the right cheek and then on the left cheek and went alone through the yard to my little room. The green and yellow bedspread that had kept me company for many summers greeted me.

"How We Met": An Interview with Gloria Steinem and Robin Morgan

by Angela Neustatter
For *The Independent,* 1992

GLORIA STEINEM: I remember I used to think it quite in order for a woman friend to cancel an arrangement with me to go out with a man, because it was so obviously preferable. As women became more integrated into society this century, men became the priority, the people women would choose to be with in preference to their own sex. But through feminism, friendship between women has now grown into something absolutely central to their lives. My friends—and Robin very particularly—are my chosen family, and I feel that, as we get older, this chosen family is going to be at the heart of life, as valuable as the families we are born into or create, and in some cases more so.

I first spoke to Robin on the phone at the end of the sixties, when I was doing an article on the women's movement for *New York* magazine, but we didn't meet until we were both on a panel with other women involved in feminist politics. She was reading her poem, "Monster," with such ferocity that it frightened me. I was always accepting invitations and then backing off because I couldn't face public speaking. Robin seemed so totally absorbed and unselfconscious.

We came together at almost the beginning of *Ms.* Robin came into the office to see what she could contribute. She became a contributing editor, so we became close through the work we were doing, and through sharing the euphoria at what was going on among women. As the best friendships do, ours developed and grew out of a conviction that the politics we were involved in mattered so much.

When Robin's marriage broke up after twenty years, I was well aware of the pain she was in and that she needed me to be there. I don't know many women who subscribe to the idea that all men should be dropped off the edge of the planet—as feminists have so often been portrayed—but I did find myself going crazy with the unfairness of Robin's situation. She'd spent years nurturing her family, supporting her husband, and doing incredible work—yet here she was, suffering hardship and needing somewhere to go.

When Robin fell in love with a woman after her marriage ended, it could have altered the tenor of our friendship, which is what has happened with other people who've made the same journey. I think the difference was that Robin was authentically falling in love with a person who happened to be a woman, not acting out a dissatisfaction with men, or some political position. Equally, if she'd then become critical of my heterosexuality, it would have changed our friendship. But that's just never happened. I've wondered how it would be if Robin were suddenly not there, and believe I'd feel bereft and as though some vital warning system about life's emergencies was gone. Robin doesn't threaten or bully me, but she's like a warm and pleasant version of a life-threatening accident.

When we're both in New York we see each other two or three times a week. We go to the movies, out for meals—we both love food, and we have a regular "wimmin's" dinner for five of us. The other thing we do is go to the gigs given by the rock band in which Robin's son plays. I don't know what the rest of the audience makes of this bizarre bunch of graying groupies clapping and singing along.

ROBIN MORGAN: When I was organizing the first Miss America Pageant protest in 1968, Gloria rang me to talk about this women's movement thing. Though she had to ask all sorts of quite hostile questions to please her editor, she apologized for this, and it was clear that she understood immediately what it was all about. So there was a connection.

But what really caught me with Gloria was an extraordinary act of kindness. We were due to do a discussion together with a panel. I was onstage, and Gloria smiled and rather shyly slid me a manila envelope, saying "I've some friends over at the TV network, and I asked them to pull these. I thought you might prefer that they're not floating around." Inside the envelope were photos of me as an apple-cheeked, curly-haired child star. My parents put me into acting, and though I got out in my teens, the press kept digging out these pictures and writing about them as a way of trivializing my politics.

I've felt very protective toward Gloria recently with the publication of her book *Revolution from Within*. She had the courage to be vulnerable and questioning in it. But she's been attacked for betraying the women's movement because she was supposed to be this perfect icon who mustn't reveal human fallibility. It's wildly unfair.

Gloria is often thought of as strident and forceful, but in fact she's peaceful, serene, and midwestern. She comes from a very understated background. I come out of an apostate Jewish New York context, in which exaggeration is almost an art form. Sometimes I really want a confrontation, because that's my nature. Gloria can drive me bananas at times, because she's prepared to suffer fools gladly, and I'm not. You could say I appear to be hyperventilating all the time, and she might seem catatonic. But together we're a great balance and we make a complete person.

Gloria can make me laugh like no one else. She has a

wonderful humor and a genius for aphorisms. She jokes that she decided not to have children when she realized she didn't have to. Her mother had a nervous breakdown when Gloria was young, and she spent much of her childhood mothering her mother, so I feel she's done that and doesn't want it again in adult life. But she's wonderful with my son, Blake, and one of those people we mothers turn to because they have so much to give our kids.

Gloria was a friend beyond sisterhood during the most difficult personal period in my life. My mother was dying after a long illness, my marriage of twenty years was ending, and *Sisterhood Is Global*—which had been thirteen years in the making—was coming to completion. I was also broke, as I'd been supporting my mother, my husband, and my child. When we split up, I needed a place to stay, and [I needed] support. Gloria was there giving it—whether offering the keys to her home, a loan of money, sanity and peace, or an ear when I needed it.

She also gave me the best support when I fell in love with the woman I've been living with for ten years. Some of my women friends became very nervous, thinking that if it could happen to me, it could happen to them—and their husbands became still more nervous! Others perceived it as a failure or rebound from my marriage. Gloria didn't bat an eyelash, but just asked whether I was in love. Was this person being good to me? She accepted it absolutely and acted as she would have about any new lover.

Conversely, I've picked her up on a few occasions when her relationships have caused suffering. I've attempted not to be judgmental although there was one man she became involved with whom I thought so unpleasant I couldn't disguise it. When it ended, we were able to laugh about that together.

The serious side of our friendship is our mutual passion for the cause and our political involvement. It's involved a good deal of sacrifice, delightedly given, of time that we might have spent writing and expressing that side of our creativity. But there's a jokey, playing side as well: we laugh about the obsession we share for the same pencils, which must be sharpened in the right way. And we both care for cats and dolphins. The only thing that would wreck our friendship would be if Gloria went on a self-destruct course so that she went right away from the things we hold dear.

Kat

by Guinevere Turner

Guinevere Turner grew up in the Lyman Family, a group of 150 people that formed in Boston in the mid-sixties, led by Mel Lyman. Later, communities were formed in Los Angeles, Kansas, Martha's Vineyard, San Francisco, and New York. In 1974 a reporter from Rolling Stone *visited the Lyman Family for a week and wrote an article about them. The family members were so upset with the article, which portrayed them as a cult and compared them to the Manson family, that they took all of their children out of public schools and made all contact with the outside world as minimal as possible. In the past ten years they have built a house in Mexico, and the birth of several children has marked the beginning of the family's third generation.*

You can't imagine what I felt like when I recognized Kat. The feeling raced up my legs and hit the top of my skull. The embrace I threw around her was one of the few truly spontaneous embraces I have given in my adult life. It took a few moments for me to remember that I was a lesbian and she probably was not—we were two girls of ten. My knees were muddy, and her hair was in braids. She was in trouble, and her twin sister was not. She was washing and I was standing on a chair putting the dishes away. I was watching her be paddled in front of all the other kids for leaving her clothes in the fields, laughing to myself because, just like me, she had on ten pairs of underwear. She was screaming at the leech on my leg.

A friend of mine says "Guin, there's someone here who says she grew up with you." I laugh. No one grew up with me. I grew up on another planet and I'm the only one who's not still on that planet. She leads me to Kat. Kat says "Guinevere?" I stare blankly. "It's Kat. It's me. Katherine."

"Katie?" And I leaped on her.

Kat and I grew up in a Family of 150 people—"The Family." We didn't go to public school, and we didn't listen to the radio. The only television shows we saw were old movies that we were required to watch. At night we all sat around and sang while the adults played instruments. It was a highly intolerant, manipulative, and frightening place to grow up, but we didn't know that. It was our lives for as long as we could remember, and we were taught to believe that we were being protected from the World. And from World People. We were taught to work on our souls, to believe in Mel Lyman, whose photograph was everywhere on our walls, to learn about his life, and above all to work and try to understand. The Earth was school, and we were lucky children to be in the Family that was going to be saved from it. Someday, someday, we would all be taken to Venus. We traveled across the country in a school bus that said "Venus or Bust" on the side and believed that until each one of us was perfect, no one was going. For the first time in fifteen years, I'm standing in front of someone who doesn't find that the slightest bit funny.

I am gripped with the idea suddenly that it is imperative for her to know I'm queer. "So you're called Guin now?" she says. "No one calls you Jenny?"

I say, "And you're Kat?" We laugh a knowing laugh together, and I picture us standing in line at Ellis Island. Then

I'm terrified. I can't tell her. She'll close off. She'll shrink away. I couldn't bear that. I want to devour this woman, to trade guts.

We're in a bar in the East Village, and she is the bartender. She walks away and I watch her pour a beer for someone and my joy is overwhelming. Look at how she passes, see her pretend. You'd never know in a million years. Just like me. You'd never know.

I entertain a fantasy that she's also queer—that she's just nervous about telling me because we were both taught that man is great, that woman was created to help him to greatness, that homosexuality is akin to uselessness, and above all, that if you're homosexual you have no soul. If you have no soul there's no way to love Mel Lyman. She's as worried about how much of this I believe as I am. If only she was. Oh, how much of my life I could project onto her and read through her.

She returns, and we just keep smiling at each other. The music is loud. She says, "I heard you made a movie or something."

I say, "Yeah, I did." I am suddenly aware of all the dykes I came in with, and I hate them because I feel exposed by them. And yet I want to take Kat's hand and jump up on the bar and say, "We grew up in a commune! A cult! A big fucking crazy Family!" and just say "we" over and over again because it feels so much better than "I."

I plunged. "Do you know what my movie's about?"

"Gay people or something?"

I look her in the eye and say, "Yes. It is." Then I chicken out and look at the performers onstage. Then I peek back at her.

"Are *you* gay?" She asks innocently, as if the idea occurred to her in that second, and I believe it did.

"Yes. I am."

"Cool." She draws out the word a little, bobbing her head.

I am frantic trying to read this one word. I am frantic in trying not to appear frantic, and trying to feel as rock-solid in my identity as I did when I walked into this bar. In that moment I am a traitor to all queerness—I want desperately for her to fall in love with me the way that I have with her, and I would trade queerness and probably a limb to have her accept me, and to be able to touch her again without the word "gay" or "cool" hanging in the air.

We belong in the Family. We belong together with the hordes of other children we grew up with. We are out here because we are lost souls. We found each other because the Family has that power, because in the end we all belong together. My sexuality seems incidental to this monumentous truth, and in a flash I wonder if it was just an attempt to regain the Family that I lost. A decision I made so I could feel huge arms around me that say, "Within these boundaries you are safe." The feeling I get when I see a dyke in the street and our eyes meet knowingly is the same feeling I get when I look into Kat's eyes. We know. The desperation for acknowledgment is the same. The strength it gives is immeasurable.

There's no more to this story. She told me rave culture saved her life when she first got out, and we danced, just the two of us, until four o'clock in the morning. We didn't talk much because there was too much to say. Someone asked her where she was from, and I said, "Yeah, Kat, where *are* you from?" and we laughed like little girls.

Did I imagine that she danced for me? Did she feel my eyes on her and all of that confused desire?

One thing is this: neither of us put the barrier there. It's there the minute you say what you are, and it doesn't matter how the other person actually feels or what she does. The torture is waiting for you. Does she think I want her? Can I say this without scaring her? Is she repulsed by me? Intrigued? I wanted to hold her hand all night and maybe sneak and see how she smelled, but of course I didn't.

Later I thought if I wasn't a lesbian I would have known what to do, how to spill it all out to her and tell her that this evening had changed my life forever. How to ask her never to leave me. But there was all that madness in the way.

I cried all the way home.

Like Cutting Off My Arm

by Sylvia Brownrigg

We laughed, we laughed everywhere together. We mapped out a small colorful universe with our laughter.

We were best friends. It had been a while since I'd had one. I was just eighteen—we both were—and I'd forgotten the strength and joy of that companionship. I had other friends, friends who seemed more adult and sophisticated, political friends: cool friends. This friendship cut through all those pretensions, reached straight back to childhood. We brought each other candy (I remember a bag of Raisinets pinned to my door). We rubbed each other's heads when they were sore and tired. We left cryptic notes for each other in coded languages, in the Mandarin she was learning, in our own private girlspeak. We didn't talk about sex.

It was our first year in college, a place we had come to from separate and not quite equal geographies. Nell was from the South and I was from the West, while the college was all East Coast, as East Coast as they get. Nell talked to me in a disguised Southern accent and with some inherited familiarity with the elite college landscape we inhabited; I brought a blond open-faced exoticism to this place and even to her life, I think—I was that strange, interesting creature, a Californian.

Our friendship formed fast. In the first crucial months we spent hours talking until late, dancing frantically at parties, meeting in the middle of the night. We lingered in the dining hall and lounged in the library, laughing at other people. We sent packages to each other's homes at Christmas. We listened to Bob Marley, mellowly, in each other's rooms as we philosophized with the new grandeur of college freshmen. We talked about being related, somehow. We felt like sisters to each other.

But then something started to happen to me, and I began to peel away from Nell. I started to want to think about sex and to talk about it. This was something we couldn't do. If we were flirting with boys, and we were, they were distant, unsexed creatures whom neither of us took very seriously. But also there was the problem of politics. My new cool friends were feminists. They were also gay. At first I wanted to be a feminist too—Nell was indifferent; she was playing hockey; she had other things to think about—though I was clear that that didn't mean I was necessarily a lesbian. Soon it was clear that I was, as I put it to myself, "at least" a lesbian and that I wanted that whole life. Eventually I wanted a particular woman in that life, an out lesbian several years older than I was, a grown-up, so it seemed to me. I had fallen in love for the first great time.

I still loved Nell, but the distance grew painful. My political life took up a lot of time, as did her life of academic studies and a social world that was connected to her Southern background. It's probably significant that I can't remember when I told her about my new love or how that conversation unfolded. What I do remember is her spending those spring months trying to convince me that my lover was evil, or certainly unstable. Nell thought I was making a great mistake.

Then, unforgivably, when her parents showed up for a rare visit to the campus and I was slated to meet them, I somehow couldn't make it. I made some poor excuse to Nell when in fact I was wrapped in the arms of my lover at the time, choosing in some basic rebellious way my lesbian life over the conventional heterosexual one of the parents—*all* parents—whom I was escaping.

Nell's parents, with whom she was still close, began around this time issuing warnings to her that I was a feminist and probably dangerous. I don't think she'd yet told them I was a lesbian, but she eventually would—prompted by her mother intercepting some mail I'd sent to her at home, which may have included indiscreet details about my life.

That summer we were far apart, and frankly Nell was not the first thing on my mind. I was away from my lover and missing her horribly. Worse, I was at home with my mother and stepfather, and I decided abruptly and probably prematurely to come out to them. My mother did not take the news well. It was a summer of pain, though those opening skirmishes with my mother would turn out later to be only the fairly mild beginnings of a bloody seven- or eight-year war we had over my being gay. Into this summer, like water on a fat fire, streamed letters from Nell, who from the religious enclave of her home in the South was writing to me about how wrong it was to be gay and how I didn't have to choose this life and how I shouldn't.

I can still physically remember the shaking in my hands and voice the first time I saw Nell again after that summer. We ran into each other near the post office back at college. We both had our new lives to get back to: hers with a mostly straight and eclectic set, mine with the campus radicals. But the friendship, love, fear, and anger—our shared versions of betrayal—already made the air hot between us and left me with an empty, sinking stomach. I loved her still, my body told me. We made a lunch date for a few days later, knowing we had things to talk about.

We sat at lunch together in the relative privacy of an off-campus restaurant-bar and we watched each other. There was no laughter.

What I didn't know was that Nell had something to tell me. What she had to tell me was that her parents had forbidden her to be friends with me. They were very clear about it. She was no longer allowed to see me or talk to me, and they threatened to disown her if she did.

I was, what? Too dangerous; a lesbian; trying to turn her into a lesbian, too; trying to seduce her and probably ruin her morally and/or physically. Her father said being gay was unnatural—an act against God—and that gay people were diseased, like rats with fleas.

Why did Nell go along with this injunction? Her parents were a thousand miles away or so. How could they know if we still talked to each other? But the point was somehow that Nell wanted to be part of my punishment. It was clear that she still loved me. This wasn't a scene in which someone's deep revulsion twists her face, in which the hatred and rejection are deep in her heart—whatever mangled kind of heart that is. Nell told me that she wanted very much to be friends with me still, that there was nothing she wanted more. She said that if it weren't for this terrible decision I'd made in my life, we could be so happy, our friendship restored, our closeness perfect.

By now we had left the restaurant and were walking back to the campus. We were on a sidewalk.

"It is like cutting off my right arm to lose you like this."

That's the line of hers I remember from our strange, tearful goodbye on the sidewalk. I also remember the pain. It was a pain that shredded my insides, making me wonder if this was bound to be the consequence of my new kind of life. After all, I'd also just begun to lose my mother for the same reason.

Later there was rage, of course. I had a lover who loved me as well as a supportive political community who would, without my even asking them to, defend me from my sexist father and from my mother's angry taunts and from this friend, this retrograde southerner who acted out this old morality, this bigotry, this homophobia. My other pals and my lover would mock Nell and tell me to forget her. What I remember, though, is the pain. And that this seemed to be a price of my new life. The pain was real—it was for a friendship that had been genuine and deep to me, it was the pain of losing something you need, it was like cutting off my right arm.

A lot of people weren't surprised several years later when Nell became involved with another woman.

You'd think I would have been one of those people who were not surprised. But in fact I *was* a little surprised. I have a crazy tendency to believe what people tell me. So over those years when we somehow got back on reasonable terms—I guess she felt that a thousand miles was enough distance, after all, though she never mentioned my name to her parents again—and Nell kept insisting to me that she was interested in men—there was one she even thought briefly of marrying—I was supportive and I believed her. I did this on the condition that she'd cut short her continuing efforts to convince me that being gay was wrong. I think I supported these men in Nell's life—she hardly ever seemed excited about them; it was usually her friendships with women that lit up her eyes—because I thought she would keep me connected to the heterosexual world I'd moved so far away from. I wanted to be open-minded. I didn't want to be narrow and live a narrow life, as my mother threatened I surely would, with my choices.

Also, though, I'd never really believed in that lesbian habit of sizing someone up and saying, "She just hasn't figured it out yet." This was a common line in our gay community then, and I didn't, and still don't, like the condescension in it. (The head lesbian on campus at the time, who often spoke that way, singled out Nell as such an example of a "proto-dyke."

They had a disagreement over the question, to put it mildly.)
So when Nell became involved with women after college, I
wasn't even that tempted to say, "Aha! You see?" It was more
important to me that she apologize meaningfully for the
heart-ripping period in which she had disowned me as her
friend. I watched her live at first a cautious, discreet life in
the shadow of her home community, and I wondered at the
decisions she'd made.

Several years later our friendship became solid again
when our geographies met. It's another scene I can remember in my body. We had both moved and changed and suffered and ended up, as you might expect, in San Francisco.
Nell and I ran around in a park at the top of a hill, playing
tennis. It was good to feel the companionship moving
through my arms again. It was, after all, much as it had always been—there was a connection between us that was
deep, that didn't have to do with being similar but had to do,
somehow, with being kin.

Later that day we were in the apartment in Russian Hill
that Nell shared with her lover, another professional woman.
By now Nell was wielding a good deal of power in the corporate world, while I was straggling along, trying to write,
trying to teach, trying to get over another breakup. I sat in the
kitchen of this new couple and watched as the two women
became, in each other's company and in the privacy of their
home, two giggling girls, speaking a private language,
prompting each other through mysteries I'd forgotten to a
deep laughter, a laughter that covered everything, that excluded everyone in the world but the two of them. I remember watching them and laughing too because of the contagion
of it but also knowing that that laughter wasn't really mine.

I didn't know whether to be envious or not of Nell and her
lover. The girlish connection between them seemed wonderful and frightening to me. The relationship I was then
painfully disentangling myself from had had that kind of
childlike element in it—the two of us sharing secrets against

the world, making our laughing way together through cities
and parks and families—that element had somehow proved
dangerous for me. It had ripped me up when it ended. My
lover had gotten too far in. My lover was there in a place
where Nell had once been, I think, many years before, when
the connection between two young women was still safe and
sexless and we could play music in each other's rooms and
rub each other's heads with a strange innocence, something
like simplicity.

In that same imaginative place Nell had her girlfriend,
now. Nell and I were still close, still good, deep friends, but
we weren't *best* friends, the kind you have in grade school. Is
it tough for gay women to have other lesbians as best
friends? I don't know. We sat in that kitchen and we all
laughed, but my laughter wasn't in the same world as theirs,
which only had room for two.

I moved. I was always moving. Always moving and always, it
seems now, entering into a new—the idea was for it to be improved—relationship.

Time passes. I loved and lost, again. Nell met this lover
just once, though we were together for over three years. We
met at a restaurant for dinner, the four of us—my lover and
me, Nell and the same girlfriend I'd first met in San Francisco. They still lived together, and both had become even
more successful in their careers.

My lover then was very good-looking. In one great moment, putting on a boardroom manner—she'd gotten used to
being corporate—Nell pulled me aside at the dinner table
and admired my taste in women, I think somehow even com-
plimented me for "catching" her. Nell and her girlfriend
weren't quite as ecstatically gigglesome as they had been before, but they had a solidness, that deep childlike link, that
my lover and I lacked. I prided myself in this relationship on
finally having found a perfectly *adult* way of relating to
someone. None of this baby talk, this lack of clarity. My

lover and I spoke in whole sentences to each other, which seemed important to us. We were articulate. (Other close lesbian friends my age—late twenties—knew what I meant and wanted that too; we were all trying to grow up.) Two years later, after traveling together, after setting up a home together, she and I split up. I guess we discovered that for all our clear conversations and compatible careers and mutual respect—we weren't kin. Never had been.

It was after this that Nell, my old old friend, came to see me in my newest, so-called permanent, solitary home. We had been friends by now for over a decade.

Nell and her girlfriend had stayed together through the ups and downs of San Francisco life. What was I doing, besides still scraping together a writing career? I was finally— ten years after coming out, ten years after being likened to my friend's amputated arm and, by my mother, to a form of cancer—questioning the whole thing, questioning all of it. Wondering if women were worth it. Wondering if I'd ever get the *right* language with a woman, a language that would last, a language that could be warm and excited without infantilizing us both, that could be adult without being cold and detached. I wanted someone I could laugh with. I was thinking, I told Nell as we walked in the park, about seeing men. I'd had an intense crush on a man recently. One or two brief affairs.

She didn't take the news well. It was an effort for Nell to remember what the appeal of a man, any man, could be. We talked and talked as we walked around the park. She had been depressed about work, and I'd listened to her in her deep depression, so she wanted to do me the favor of listening to me, too. But the dogmatist in her was still there. She was still reluctant to let me out of the fold. (It was a different fold, of course, from the one of ten years before.) Of the various gay friends I'd talked to about these thoughts, she was one of the most incredulous that I could really be suggesting the possibility of this sexual shift.

She held on, though. Nell did listen. I don't even know what I was saying, in the end. These questions, in the absence of a real passion, become abstract, meaningless. There was no particular man to hold up for Nell's opinion or approval— there was just the *idea* of men, the idea, ironically, of something different. Now I'm not sure whether I was really arguing for being bisexual or just trying to work out what had gone wrong between me and the women I'd chosen as lovers. Whichever it was, Nell tried to be supportive.

The important thing for us was feeling our friendship as strong, strange, and deep as ever. As ever, our conversations weren't like any I had had with other friends. We don't talk to each other out of shared lives or shared interests or shared politics. We still don't talk about sex. Instead we talk and move and laugh out of some early and permanent recognition, a recognition of each other that cuts through the obvious differences between us. I don't know if we'd still describe the other as a sister. Since those first headiest days of our friendship and the great shifts and dramas that followed, we are maybe more like cousins. But who, besides people in your family, can you disown so absolutely then reclaim a few years later? Who else can you not see for years and then pick up and laugh with, call in the middle of the night?

Nell and I took pictures of each other in the park over the few days we walked there. The first ones are black-and-white pictures Nell took of me, mostly standing against a brick wall, my shoulders slumped a little shyly, a self-conscious but affectionate October smile on my face. Later there are color pictures I took of her. A couple of her with a cigar in her mouth, posing boldly, a cigar she was smoking in celebration of her love for her girlfriend. Then there are a couple that are purely Nell, purely my friend, running across a patch of park with both arms outspread, with the abandon of a child, flying whole into the unseen future of the following frame. You can hear me laughing from behind the camera.

Working Out

by Harriet Brown

The air was fragrant with dirty feet, mildew, and sweat. My sister and I busied ourselves with keys, opening the long metal lockers and slipping off our street shoes. This was our first morning together in almost two years, and we were spending it at the health club.

Kasey hadn't been to my home in almost ten years, although we had seen each other in the meantime in California, where she lives, and in New Jersey, where our parents used to live. I was excited about her visit. I was also nervous. What would we *do* for four whole days? Then I remembered the health club I had recently joined. If all else fails, I thought, we can work out.

And so we packed our gym bags on a glorious Indian summer morning, the last of the warm weather before the long Wisconsin winter set in. I parked the car and led my sister into the health club. I've only been to a couple of other health clubs, but they seem interchangeable to me. They all have the same stale air, the same fluorescent lights, the same throbbing boom-boom-boom of aerobics-class music.

The irony of our visit was rich. My sister and I grew up in a household made chaotic by emotion, and we each responded to it in a different way. Through the years of our childhood we inhabited opposite sides of the mind-body dichotomy. I was the brain, she was the brawn. I skipped grades, she skipped classes. I broke records, she broke fingers playing softball and volleyball, all ten of them at various times and occasionally at the same time. All through elementary school she was easy to spot in a crowd because she always had at least one finger taped into a big metal splint, poking upward in a kind of permanent fuck you.

While we were growing up, we lived up to our stereotypes—the jock and the geek—even as we longed to shed them, even as we longed to truly get to know each other. Eventually we did both, and discovered that we actually liked each other. Now, in our mid-thirties, there are still plenty of differences between us, but they matter less. Kasey likes disco, I like folk. She believes in reincarnation, I am a practicing Quaker. She loves women, I love men. So what? We're sisters. That's what counts.

There is one way in which we still play out our childhood roles. Out in Oakland my sister is a regular at Gold's Gym, where she lifts weights, does bench presses and crunches, and sweats on the StairMaster. She pumps iron with the hardbodies, the (mostly) men who spend hours every day enlarging this muscle and that and admiring their own sweat-polished torsos. Whereas my idea of fun is lying in a steaming bathtub with a pint of Ben & Jerry's and a book. I had only just joined the health club in an effort to lose some weight.

Down in the locker room, my sister and I started to undress. "You know what this reminds me of?" I asked her. "Changing for eighth grade gym class. You had to take your clothes off and put those dopey-looking bloomers on without anyone seeing your bra, if you were lucky enough to wear one. Remember?"

No answer. I looked up from lacing my shoes and saw my sister trying to pull down her pants with one hand while the other clutched a towel to her bare shoulders. A wave of pinkness flooded her face. My sister was *embarrassed*. I couldn't believe it. My own sister was embarrassed to be naked in front of me. My sister, who is always pointing out hot-looking women to me and describing in great detail what makes them hot—now suddenly Ms. Modesty?

We finished getting dressed in silence, our backs primly turned toward each other. Straight women always look, checking each other's bodies out in the locker room, a function of sexual competitiveness. Those sidelong glances create an instant sense of hierarchy: She's thinner, I'm curvier. But my sister and I have rarely competed in this way. Our competitiveness has always taken a different form: who got more money for her birthday, who got to go to the baseball game with Dad. There was a sexual element to this competitiveness, but it had more to do with our parents' attitude toward our sexuality than with our own. When I was a teenager, our mother found birth control pills in my purse, and the ensuing uproar sent me out of the house forever. When my sister was a teenager, she slept with her girlfriends in our parents' house. Once, in fact, our grandmother opened the door to Kasey's room while she was making love to a woman. Our grandmother paused, said, "Excuse me," and retreated, closing the door behind her. Some time later she sent my sister a copy of *The Well of Loneliness*.

As adults, Kasey and I don't often discuss our sexuality. Years ago, when I was living in New York and she was at home with our parents, she made strict rules about which of my friends I could and couldn't tell that she was gay. But she had long since outgrown that adolescent mixture of shame and pride. Nowadays I know which of my sister's relationships broke up because her partners didn't like sex. She knows which of my relationships dragged on just *for* the sex. We don't talk details, though, and I have no idea whether that's unusual. Do sisters who share the same sexual orientation talk about technique—or do they also veer away from the nitty-gritty?

As we stuffed our street clothes into the lockers, I suddenly wondered how it would feel to be undressing in front of Kasey if she were a man—if she were my brother instead of my sister. I knew the answer right away: Awful. Uncomfortable. That thought gave me pause. *Why* would it be uncomfortable? Because my "brother" would be looking at me the way he looked at other women, sexually appraising me? Because I was looking at him the same way? Maybe, for Kasey, undressing in front of me felt equally uncomfortable. Maybe on some level I had never really acknowledged her sexuality, putting aside the specifics of her relationships with women. Maybe now that we were learning to know each other, I wanted to believe she was as much like me as possible. Now she was making it clear that she was not.

Once we left the locker room, my sister's color and manner returned to normal. The health club was full of people, as it almost always is. The other women all wore spandex tights and leotard thongs that crept up their backsides, the kind of clothes that showed every wiggle and jiggle. Not us, I thought. Our clothes, by sisterly coincidence, were almost identical: shorts, oversized T-shirts, and sneakers.

Kasey had promised to teach me some exercises for developing arm muscles. One of her friends is a personal trainer, so she knows about these things the way I know about sentence fragments and stories. We entered the exercise room, an enormous rectangular space with floor-to-ceiling mirrors on every wall, many of which had a circuslike propensity to distortion. At one end were the StairMasters and exercise bikes. The other end, where we were headed, was where the hardbodies congregated to lift, press, and preen. We passed a cluster of men wearing wide leather weight belts and fingerless gloves. They carried towels and spray bottles of disinfectant—for cleaning sweat off the machines, I presume. Neither of us gave them a second glance. That was one thing we had in common—neither of us was the slightest bit interested in men with inflated body parts.

I had always avoided this end of the room, feeling ill at ease and flabby among the pumped-up bodies. (I'd also wondered how grown men had the time to do nothing but lift weights all day.) But Kasey swaggered through the room, casting a critical eye on the equipment. From time to time she shook her head or clucked her tongue, clearly unimpressed. Finally she found a few machines that sufficed, and we began my lesson. She taught me exercises for my pecs, delts, abs, quads, and hams and then threw in biceps and triceps for good measure.

Next we moved on to free weights, where Kasey demonstrated the crab and other assorted moves that had my tongue hanging out in no time. After that we did aerobics, climbing, biking, and walking to nowhere for half an hour. Finally it was time for floor exercises. We lay down side by side on the mats. I did thirty sit-ups, cursing to keep my spirits up. Then I lay flat on my back.

"Tired?" my sister asked.

"I'm doing Kegels," I replied.

My sister had never heard of Kegels—no wonder, since she'd never had a baby. Kegels—named, no doubt, after some male doctor—are designed to tone your pelvic floor muscles, which you don't even realize you have until they're ripped apart when you give birth. If they're flabby or floppy or otherwise not in the best of shape, you have some control over urination, but not enough—a plight common to new mothers.

I explained to Kasey what Kegels were and how to do them, then wickedly enjoyed watching her try to find the right muscle. "You're supposed to do two hundred a day," I said. "But I hate them. That's why I never did them after Anna was born. Then last year I got bronchitis, and every time I coughed I peed in my pants. I couldn't keep up with the laundry."

My sister laughed. "Some people say you can do these anywhere," I continued. "On a bus, driving a car, in a meeting with your boss. Personally, I have trouble carrying on a coherent conversation while I'm squeezing my vaginal muscles in and out." A woman with a finely sculpted body, on an exercise bike near us, turned and stared. My sister and I looked at each other and then collapsed into hysterics, laughing as children do at their own bad jokes.

The rest of my sister's visit went fine—more than fine. We really connected. As I stood at the bus stop a few days later, waving at her face in the darkened bus window, I realized that for the first time her leaving felt like a loss, as if a part of me were leaving too. Something had eased between us, like a muscle coming unkinked. Afterward you rub at the place that remembers the pain and wonder why it took you so long to realize it hurt.

Before she got on the bus, my sister gave me a piece of paper. There, in her untidy handwriting, were the exercises she had shown me. I held it in one hand as I hugged her goodbye, as I stood watching her bus dwindle and disappear around the corner. Changing in the locker room after our workout, we had without comment averted our eyes from each other's bodies, wrapping ourselves in towels. And when we finally left the health club, our identical heads of curly black hair slicked back and gleaming in the sun, I had had a kind of epiphany. All those years I had thought of my sister as my opposite—a beloved opposite, but an opposite nonetheless. Now suddenly I could see how alike we were, in all the ways that mattered.

I folded the paper she had given me and put it in my pocket. By the time I dug it out, weeks later, the words would be gone, bleached out in the wash, the paper soft and pliable. It didn't matter, though. Everything between us would work out just the same.

2

Romantic Love

Can't Help It

by Sarah Schulman

I was born Rita Anne Weems in Jackson Heights, Queens, New York City, U.S.A., on August 1, 1959. My father, Eddie Weems, fixed couches for the Castro Convertibles Corporation. My mother, Louisa Rosenthal Weems, was one of those hollowed-out blond beauties who made their way to New York via Thereisenstadt and then a displaced persons' camp. There are a lot of them still walking around. I see them on the subways now and then. But in Jackson Heights, where I grew up, they were a dime a dozen.

My mother smoked four packages of Chesterfields a day and died of cancer when I was ten. My memories of her are stained nicotine yellow and accompanied by a deep, painful hacking cough. Officially I've given up smoking. I rarely buy a pack. But some days I just do it. The privacy of a good smoke on a cold day. Feeling awkward around a table. Talking on the phone. Then, at night, I'll lie in bed clutching my breasts, my lungs, that hole in my chest where the burning smoke sits. My mind rolls over as I beg and beg for redemption.

When I pray, I pray to the Jewish God. I pray to the patri-

archal God who is not an energy or a spirit but an old white
man with a beard who sits up there deciding things. My
mother prayed to him. My grandmother prayed to him, and
as far as I'm concerned, that is reason enough. We exist together in that moment of panic where my thoughts turn up to
the sky.

My first job was cashier. Then I cleaned up a Catholic
school cafeteria. All those girls in green plaid kilts with dusty
white skin and matching white food. Instant mashed pota-
toes. Instant vanilla pudding. In my senior year I started
working at J. Chuckles on Forty-second Street in Manhattan.
There I earned enough money to buy a camel's-hair coat.

My mother, Louisa Rosenthal, was born in Bremen and lost
everything during the war. I, Rita, am named for her mother.
My brother Howie is named for her father, and my brother
Sam is named for her brother. Rest in peace. She married my
dad, a Catholic. But my mother was a person who could not
care about things like propriety. She just went through the
motions. What could the neighbors do to her now?

"Your mother liked the worst," my dad said a hundred thousand times. "She liked bratwurst, teawurst, and knockwurst."

But he pronounced it "woist" like Huntz Hall in those old
Dead End Kids movies. That's the way most white people in
Queens actually talk.

My mother was the most beautiful woman in the world.
She had that fragile German movie-star sensuality. She had
blue eyes and soft lips. Her mouth was shapely. Her hair was
fine and bright. But her eyes were nothing, flat. That worked,
though, for the complete beautiful-victim look. I have a photograph of her in a suit with shoulder pads; it was taken when
she first came to New York and was employed as a clerk at
Woolworth's. She had thick lipstick and pale, empty eyes. On
the way to work, some fashion photographer saw her on the
bus and invited her into his studio to take a few pictures. Her
face was slightly twisted. She held a sultry cigarette.

"Your mother was like Marilyn Monroe," my father said.
"A real doll."

There are a few other photographs. Louisa and Eddie at Niagara Falls. Louisa and Eddie at Rockaway Beach . Louisa and Eddie eating a Kitchen Sink ice cream sundae at Jahn's Ice Cream Parlour. The kids are in that one too. Me, age three, sitting on my father's lap. Sam, age seven, happy, benign, acting just the way kids are supposed to act. Howie, age ten, looking to the side at the wrong moment, ice cream all over his shirt.

Here is one of the classic Weems family stories. It stars me, age two, sitting in the stroller at the German deli where Louisa bought her teawurst.

"I'm not happy," I reportedly announced in a booming bawl.

"Why not?" Mr. Braunstein asked from behind the counter.

"I'm not happy," I repeated. "Because my daddy isn't here."

Where was he? Off in a car full of tools to some richer person's more expensive house in a better neighborhood of Queens like Kew Gardens or Forest Hills or someplace in Manhattan or out on the island, the North Shore. He held the nails in his mouth and spit them out into place. He carried a hammer in the sling of his work pants, thinking about the good old days in the army during the war. Mr. Handsome G.I. Listening to the crap on the car radio. My dad knew all the songs.

Now, after a night of smoking, I lie in bed, terrified.

"What am I doing with a cigarette in my hand?" I ask myself stupidly. "I've got to be out of my mind."

These days everybody is dying. Not just my mother. There's no illusion left to let a person feel immune. Invincibility is over.

I didn't get my mother's hair. Sam got it. Mine is blond and brown, sign of mixed nationalities. Howie looks even darker, real black Irish, and that's fine. But this in-between kind of washed-out blah sort of shut me down in the beauty department. I got blue eyes, true. But I also got blue skin, really pink nipples that look paraffin-coated. No pubic hair on the insides of my thighs. Thank God. Whenever you see pubic hair in a movie or a magazine, the girl's never got it down the insides of her thighs. But in real life, there's miles of it out there. There is wall-to-wall carpeting in every household in America. Some girls get embarrassed, and some act like they never noticed. But there is a discrepancy between most thighs and the ideal ones. Mine are kind of ideal.

I grew up. I got jobs, I moved far from my destiny. No husband. No night school. No screaming kids in snowsuits and strollers. No trappings. Not trapped.

My first lover was rough, knowing, leathery. She held my blue body. I was so young. I didn't know what lovemaking was. This woman was about forty, named Maria. She was sizable, weighty, assuredly handsome. I had no expectations. I couldn't give anything back. As we were doing it, I just couldn't be free. Lovemaking seemed to revolve around the shifting of weight. It had to do with climbing onto Maria's body. Her whole skeleton was involved. But when she opened my lips and put her mouth on my clitoris I couldn't react. It was too specific. The rest of me felt lonely. I was seventeen. I had no extra flesh. Maria masturbated in front of me. I sat between her legs staring like it was a television set.

After that I just started talking, blabbing on and on. I told her everything I did all day and what I was expecting to do tomorrow. I told her about every song on the radio and which ones I liked, which ones did not deserve to be hits. I told her about a time when my mother was sick and some strange-accented distant relative I'd never seen before or since took me to a store in Brooklyn to buy some clothes for the first day of school. I wore size 6X. I didn't understand why we had to go all the way to Brooklyn until we climbed up these shaky wooden stairs to the shop. The place was run by a group of friends who had been in the same concentration camp. All the clerks had numbers on their arms and screamed at each other as if they were home in their kitchens.

The second time, Maria picked me up from work and

made me keep on all my clothes. She was smart. As she passed her hands over my young breasts, there was no direct touching. No contact. That was the first time in my life that I ever felt sexy. That was the first time I ever felt that thing. Desire.

Farther down, I thought. Please put your hands farther down. I got angrier and angrier as her hands stayed in the same place.

"You've got to ask for it," she whispered. She said it like a threat. "You've got to ask for what you want."

"Put your hands down there."

"Down where?"

"In my pants."

She lifted me onto her lap and fucked me fully clothed.

"*You* are a brave young girl," she said. "You're a darling girl. Keep your clothes on and it will always feel good."

Our next and final time together, it was my turn to touch. It was an inquiry. I hadn't yet discovered shame. But Maria's cunt didn't open to my fingers the way mine had to hers. That's when I realized how trust shows in sex. It has nothing to do with how a person acts or what she says. It shows physically. I learned instinctively the telltale signs.

Being a salesgirl was a trap. That was clear from the start. Dad's new girlfriend, Erica, worked in sales, and she was obviously trapped. The staff at J. Chuckles was trapped. The manager was trapped. Even the customers were trapped by the lousy selection of overpriced clothes. I knew that I was only seventeen. I knew I was young. This job was just a moment. It was just about saving up for a camel's-hair coat. The coat was so dashing. It was substantial. It was something I had never seen before except on the back of a woman on line at Cinema One.

Saturday afternoons after work I went to Shields Coffee Shop on Lexington Avenue and had an egg salad sandwich on rye. One dollar and five cents with a pickle on the side. I sat at the counter, exhausted, and stared out the window at the people on line at Cinema One. It was New York couples

at Christmastime. The kind who went to foreign films. They
had good taste. They weren't tacky little hitters from Queens.
The girls in tight jeans and sparkle socks from my neighborhood spent their whole lives smoking Marlboros in front of
candy stores. Their boyfriends died in car accidents or never
got rid of the drug habits they'd picked up in Vietnam. Those
girls wore blue eye makeup. They listened to Elton John and
Yes and Black Sabbath at parties. They listened to *Tommy* by
The Who and Bachman-Turner Overdrive. They did
Quaaludes with their older boyfriends and then eventually
used needles and drank tequila right out of the bottle. They
never saw foreign films. I hadn't seen one either, but I would
someday. That was the difference.

Outside, the couples were standing in line. I ate my egg
salad slowly, watching. Framed by the picture window was a
distinguished older couple. The man wore a topcoat. His
wife's hair was done. She linked her arm into his. They both
looked ahead while discussing, so they could watch and comment at the same time. Behind them stood a younger version
of the older couple. The woman's cheeks blushed pink between gold earrings. The guy wore a scarf and a jacket. His
hair was long; he was hatless. Behind them stood two
women, arms linked as well. They were engaged, laughed
easily. One had to bend over slightly so the other could speak
into her ear. And then something happened that changed my
life forever. The two women kissed romantically. The one
nearest the window wore a camel's-hair coat.

The next Saturday was Christmas Day. As soon as I could
get out of the house, I took the number seven train into Manhattan, directly to Cinema One. I sat down in the virtually
empty theater and watched the same foreign film those two
women had watched. It was called *Cries and Whispers*. In it,
one woman touched another woman's face and kissed it. In
another scene a different woman bared her breasts and a
fourth laid her head on them. Then the first woman put a
piece of glass in her vagina and rubbed the blood across her
mouth. Throughout, a clock was ticking and people were

whispering in Swedish. The subtitles said, "Forgive me." I went downstairs into a stall in the ladies' bathroom and masturbated. Then I went up and watched the movie again.

That whole year my father and I were always fighting. If he told me to get out and never come back, I'd hover on the front stoop for hours screaming to get back in. If he put his foot down and told me I couldn't go out, I'd sneak down the fire escape. Our street, Eighty-second Street in Jackson Heights, was so quiet that our yelling was enough for the whole neighborhood to hear. After a few people complained, my dad got into the habit of calling the local precinct as soon as we got into a fight.

"Officer," he'd say into the telephone, "we have a girl here, out of control."

There was Spanish kids in Jackson Heights then, but not so many as now. The Spanish and the whites never mixed. That really dates me. Out on the street were good-girl German Jews coming home from their violin lessons and lots of Irish kids blaming themselves for everything starting at the age of twelve. I knew a girl who lived two apartments up from ours named Claudia Haas, and she started out as a good girl but ended up as a tramp.

My father was a rough guy. He'd already chased Howie out of the apartment and off to California somewhere to find peace and fortune. Dad's second girlfriend had dumped him, and it was taking him longer than usual to find another one, which also put him in a foul mood. So when he tossed me out for the fifteenth time, I shrugged it off and went to the candy store to buy a pack of Salems. There was Claudia Haas, tight jeans, tight V-neck short-sleeved sexy knit top. She was hanging out, a real hitter from Queens. She was drinking Mateus rosé out of the bottle and listening to Seals & Crofts on WPLJ. The real truth is that Claudia Haas fell in love with me and I fell in love with her, even though it wasn't possible on a warm Queens night in 1975 because neither of us knew what a homosexual was. That word wasn't bandied about in the newspapers then, as it is today. Even I, who had already experienced it, had never uttered the word. I had never conceptualized myself that way.

Claudia and I talked together until late that night. We sat on cars, smoked cigarettes, listened to Yes do "Close to the Edge," and fell in love. Claudia's boyfriend wore his Vietnam army jacket, turned us on to Thai weed, drank beer, listened to Grand Funk Railroad, to War, to Average White Band and Janis Ian, to the Allman Brothers singing "Whipping Post" live at the Fillmore East, to Carly Simon singing "You're So Vain," to the Stones, Emerson Lake & Palmer, Acoustic Hot Tuna, and the Dead. It was a different, stupid America. We hadn't yet given up trying to get over Vietnam. We reveled in our mediocrity. America wasn't nihilistic yet. We weren't all suffering.

That night, after we finished partying, the sky was all mine, the air warm on my skin. I followed Claudia up to her parents' tiny apartment—like ours, four rooms smashed together into a purposeful square. Remove the walls and we're all head to toe, head to toe. Her mother had left the kitchen light on, illuminating a plate of mohn kuchen, which we left untouched on the rickety table.

"Come on," Claudia whispered, leading me into the family bathroom, where we spread out towels to lie stomach down on the cool tile floor.

"What's the green stuff?" I asked.

"Herbal Essence shampoo. Smell it."

It smelled good. She had all kinds of things, special kinds of hairbrushes and sponges, powder. I never learned how to use such products. Didn't even know where to begin.

"Here, I'll brush your hair," she said pulling my hair off the back of my neck.

"I looked at these at Field's," I said. "But I didn't know what they were."

The brush felt so good against my neck, her hand there too.

Then we lay back on the floor, whispering, passing cigarettes back and forth, and blowing the smoke out through the open window.

"I'm going to Queens College in the fall," Claudia said, feet up, straight blond hair cut in a soft shag. "What about you?"

"I kind of stopped going to school," I said.

"What did your father say?"

"He hasn't mentioned it. I've been working at J. Chuckles, in the city. Is Queens College really that great?"

"My sister's been there for three years. One more and then she'll move out. After that I've got the bedroom all to myself. I got wait-listed at two other places, though, so the future is really unknown. Do you have a boyfriend?"

"Are you in love with Herbie?"

"Sure," she said. "You know what? He had this rubber last night. It said 'Put a tiger in your dot-dot-dot.' Everything's fine except there's one thing about him that I really hate."

"What's that?"

"When we're doing it—you know, balling?—sometimes he pushes my head down there because he wants a blow job. I get really pissed off. 'Don't tell me what to do.' I'm not some Vietnamese girl who has to do what he says. It's not nice."

She rolled over on her side. I was used to the dark by now, and the distant streetlights started to work for me, started to light us up. Then Claudia started singing: *Du bist sehr verrückt. Du musst nach Berlin.*

"What does that mean?"

"Don't you know German?"

"My mother forgot to teach us."

"It means," she said, brushing a piece of my hair back with her hand, "'You are so crazy, you must go to Berlin.'"

I felt her touch me, and I saw her do it as well. I saw a certain gentleness, a womanly softness as though reaching out to touch me was the most natural thing. It was 'of course.' But somewhere, barely perceptible, I detected an excitement. Something crackling.

"Fallink in luff again, nevah vanted to," she sang, taking my hand. "Vat am I to do? Cahn't help it."

lifeline

by Gloria Anzaldúa

Kika edged closer to Suel, resisting the urge to place her nose against Suel's neck and breathe in her sweet-smelling skin. They lay *lado a lado,* arms and thighs touching. Kika la Prieta was afraid of how Suel would react if she broached the subject. She couldn't decide if she should talk to Suel about *esa lumbrita,* that tiny spark she'd first seen in Suel's eyes when they met two years ago in summer session. Since then she'd caught a glimmer of it every time Suel looked at her.

They had been talking about romantic relationships they'd had in the past. Kika grappled for words to describe the air that breathed between them *cuando se sentaban juntitas.* Then she said, "Do you . . . ah, do you want to talk about it?" She stroked the soft skin on the inside of Suel's elbow. Suel pulled her arm away. She'd been touching Suel this way for weeks and Suel had never pulled away until now.

They had been up working on papers the night before. *Su cabeza* felt hollow from too much of Suel's coffee and too little sleep. *En una semana* the summer session would end and they would return to *el valle* and their respective home-towns. The more Kika thought about the 69 miles between their pueblos, the farther apart she felt from Suel. She knew their *familias* would not think it strange for friends to drive to visit each other. But they would think it strange for two women to be so close. So close that they didn't even need to talk to convey their feelings. Their eyes spoke more than words. It was different from the intimacy she had with her *novias,* yet similar.

"I want us to talk about it, Suel," Kika said.

"Talk about what?" Suel responded in a small voice, look-ing at Kika out of the corner of her eye. Kika had seen star-tled *vacas* give that same sideways glance when the cowboys came to brand them.

"I think we should maybe speak about our feelings."

"What feelings?" Suel's voice seemed sharper, and her eyes and ears seemed to flatten.

"Tú sabes. That awareness that thickens between us when we look at each other."

"Thickens? What are you talking about?" Suel said, sitting up.

"You know," Kika said, pulling back, "these, ah . . . erotic feelings."

Suel snapped her head around and stared at her. Kika felt as if her words had whipped her eyes naked, stripping off the skin veiling Suel's vulnerability. Slowly Suel edged off her bed. Then, avoiding Kika's eyes, she got up and walked out.

It hurt Kika to breathe. It felt as though she had breathed in fire and it had left red coals in her lungs. With each breath she fanned the coals. She walked from Suel's bed to peer out the window. She paced around the room. Stopped before the bookshelf. Picked up one of the small blown-glass figurines of *palomitas* that lay on the shelf. A framed Sagrado Corazón de Jesús holding two fingers over an exposed bleeding heart looked on. She stroked the tiny head of the dove and went over all the times Suel had given her signals that what she felt for Kika went beyond mere friendship. She knew Kika was a *marimacha*. So why had she acted so shocked just then?

As Kika sat on the bed, waiting for her friend to return, she remembered when she'd first seen Suel at the Food Commons while standing in the pizza line. Suel was twelve years older, tall, leggy, bordering on skinny. She walked with grace. Suel never wore makeup, she always pulled her *pelo* back in a tight bun. Kika, who was so different from her, *era chaparrita y delgada.*

They started talking and took their trays out to the patio to sit in the sun. Kika was studying how literature helped create reality, and Suel was learning how to incorporate the Mexican-American experience into the curriculum.

They were both frustrated in graduate programs and a school full of gringos. In this sea of *caras güeras,* they gravitated toward each other as to life preservers, brown buoys in a town—Austin, Texas—where Chicanos lived across the river. They sat in the air-conditioned Commons for three hours keeping each other afloat with iced drinks, *platicando de sus* courses, *sus familias,* movies, spirituality, books, everything. They got tired of talking, so they walked across the huge lawns of the UT campus, winding their way down a ravine to Waller Creek. Plopping down on a huge black rock, they sat close together and listened to the gurgle of the trickling water. As Suel leaned down to stare at the water, her arm accidentally brushed Kika's breast and she locked eyes with her. Kika noticed something naked yet veiled in her gaze before Suel dropped her eyes. Could it be? Kika wondered. Yes, desire. At the same time Kika sensed that Suel felt too vulnerable to let it show.

One hot summer day turned into another, and Kika wore a secret smile, her lips at a perpetual lift. She attributed it to Suel's presence. Suel was always poised, surrounded by calmness. Kika skirted around the edges of that calmness. She didn't have that deep quiet in her. She liked easing into that tranquillity, just as she enjoyed slipping into cool water on a hot day. Every now and then a tremor would flash through that water, leaving ripples on Kika's flesh. Like the time when Kika had asked what Suel saw in her. Suel had lowered her eyes and replied, "I like it that you surprise me. I never know what you're going to say or do. You have such strong feelings. Sometimes they . . . make me uncomfortable."

One Sunday Kika had said, *"Ay que calor.* Why don't we go and cool off at Lake Travis, Suel? The water there is nice and deep."

"I'm scared of *lo hondo,"* Suel replied.

"I'll get you a life preserver. And I'll be there to give you mouth-to-mouth—"

"Uh-uh," Suel interrupted. "Besides, I want to go to Mass."

"Bueno," Kika said, wondering why Suel felt the need to go to Mass. Religion wasn't going to wipe away Suel's awareness of her. Maybe it would give Suel the illusion of . . . finding a refuge, a place where she could hide.

The tolling of the bell atop the UT tower jerked Kika out of her reverie. She looked at her watch. An hour had passed since Suel walked out. Not wanting to fall asleep on Suel's bed in case she returned angry, Kika left.

Next day, after getting no answer when she knocked on Suel's door, Kika went to all their usual haunts: the Commons, the fountain, the drag. She questioned everyone who knew them. No one had seen Suel. Finally, after searching for days, she went to the registrar's office. She was told that Suel had had a family emergency and had left without finishing her course work. For a moment Kika thrashed in deep water, then she felt herself sinking. For the next seven days Kika forced herself to brush her teeth, go to classes, eat. She lost track of the days, was numb to the scorching Texas sun.

One night Kika lay awake for hours thinking in the dark-

ness before falling asleep. She woke up after a couple of
hours, got up to pee, and smoked while sitting on the john.
Next morning her appetite deserted her entirely. She cinched
her belt another notch. That day she walked down the *barranca* to Waller Creek and sat on their rock.

She had no interest in going out or in seeing other people.
At the end of the summer session, Kika returned to the valley. Though she knew Suel was shutting her out, Kika needed
contact with her, even if it was purely platonic. When she got
her nerve up, she called Suel's house. Suel's sister answered
and yelled out, "Suel, Kika's on the phone."

At the other end Kika heard Suel say, *"Dile que no estoy
en casa.* Tell her I moved away and I don't have a phone."

Time dragged through the fall. In the middle of winter
Kika called Suel again. She wanted to hear her voice even if
it was just to say good-bye. Her mother answered this time.
She told Kika that Suel didn't live there anymore and hung
up before Kika could ask for her address.

A year later at an in-service assembly, Kika stood at the
door of the auditorium. Her heart leaped at the sight of Suel
sitting in the middle of the huge room. She gulped in air and
felt as though she had breathed in a whole ocean. Holding in
its ebb and flow hurt her body. She remembered the empty
period she had gone through. Holding herself in, she made
straight for the row where Suel sat. She saw Suel's thin neck
under the familiar bun and felt a tenderness surge through
her body. As she approached, Suel turned her head. Kika saw
fear register in her eyes. She saw Suel leap up, rush to the
aisle, and run toward the door.

Kika felt the ocean drain out of her body in one pounding
wave, felt the lifeline slipping through her hands again, felt
the sea rise up and swallow her.

· · ·

TRANSLATIONS

Ay que calor: how hot it is
barranca: ravine
bueno: okay
caras güeras: white faces
cuando se sentaban juntitas: when they sat close together
Dile que no estoy en casa: Tell her I'm not home.
el valle: the valley
en una semana: in a week
era chaparrita y delgada: she was short and thin
esa lumbrita: that small fire
familias: families
lado a lado: side by side
lo hondo: the deep
marimacha: dyke
palomitas: small doves
pelo: hair
platicando de sus: talking about their
su cabeza: her head
Tú sabas: you know
vacas: cows

Till Men Do Us Part

by Carla Trujillo

The first time I saw Becky she was standing against the wall in the local women's bar with her arms crossed. She was with some friends and seemed to be listening to something important, because her forehead was in a scowl and her lips were pursed as if she could hardly wait to speak. When she did talk, her voice was loud. Even in the noisy bar I could hear most of what she was saying. She smiled, looked my way, and scowled again. I was a goner.

Becky, unaware of my attraction to her, virtually ignored me until she moved into an apartment I shared with another roommate. She had an outspoken manner and liked nothing better than to tell you her opinion. But beneath it all was a woman who could be wonderfully funny and playful. If the honey in the honeybear needed to be warmed up, she'd give him a bath. The little animal tchotchkes she collected would often have complete conversations about the importance of dust as they played together in it. At first she had no idea how I felt about her, but within a week she began to figure it out. Within two weeks we had fallen in love.

We both proclaimed that we had never known what it was to be in love. Both happy and frightened, Becky didn't know what to do with her fear. She would sometimes lie on her bed, rocking back and forth to comfort herself. She had only been looking for a place to call home. She had no idea that a lover would come with it.

Somehow we worked things out, calming ourselves in the routine of the day-to-day. We both went to the same university. I was in graduate school; she was working on a second degree in physical therapy. Things were blissful.

Becky was Jewish, and I was a Chicana. I had left California to attend school at a large midwestern university. There were very few people of color in the town or, for that matter, in the entire state. I was the first Chicana many folks had ever met. I often felt stereotyped. The fact that Becky was Jewish comforted me in a place where people paid extra attention to darker hair and skin. She was reassured, knowing that I had faced my share of prejudice, since she had been taught never to trust anyone who wasn't Jewish.

I missed my family and others like them. Becky's parents, though initially shy with me, eventually folded me into the family and into any consideration they gave Becky. This was at her insistence. She was an out lesbian to her family. She insisted that they respect this fact, and she wanted them to acknowledge and honor our relationship. I recall Becky getting angry when her mother sent new dishes for the house and forgot to mention me in her card. Becky never let her parents forget me. I had never been validated in a lesbian relationship before. This was a new feeling that not only felt good but made me wonderfully proud of Becky. I was not out to my father, and this—coupled with a two-thousand-mile distance and my parents' overt homophobia—compelled me to embrace Becky's family with all their love and acceptance.

Becky and I had philosophical differences stemming largely from our different class backgrounds. She was middle class and I was working class. She felt guilty that her fa-

ther was a corporate lawyer. This made her zealously politically conscious and downwardly mobile. I had been poor all
my life. The last thing I wanted was to continue living this
way. But because Becky and I came from two different
worlds, we fought over the stupidest things. I wanted a
leather couch; she wanted a futon. I liked to go car camping
with an air mattress and a big cooler filled with beer, Coke,
and meat to barbecue, while she wanted to backpack carrying nothing but bulgur, dried fruit, and water.

Still, I was very much in love with Becky. I recall going
along with her request to go birding, something I had only
seen Jane Hathaway attempt on the *Beverly Hillbillies*. I
hated hiking and found myself not only trudging through
frozen muck but also looking for birds that I would just as
happily have read about in *National Geographic*. But the excitement I felt just being with Becky was worth every step I
took. Maybe it was a bad day for birds, for we saw none. Disappointed, Becky asked if I would listen to her *Birds of the
Algonquin Marsh* album with her. I thought it would make
her happy, so I agreed. We sat beside each other, holding
hands as I tried to make out the difference between the
sound of a loon, a cormorant, and a red-throated whatever,
but they all sounded like barnyard quacks, honks, and
screeches to me. I even made an attempt to pay attention to
her accompanying narration. When the record was over, I
sighed gratefully and thought about the day. "Well, I must
like you a lot," I said to Becky. When she asked why, I told
her, "I appreciate nature, but I never thought I'd see the day
when I'd trek through mud in freezing cold weather looking
for birds I don't even care about and listening to an album
about a marsh."

She said I "wasn't in like, I was in love."

"I guess so," I replied, "but does it mean I'll have to listen
to that album again?" Luckily for me, she smiled and shook
her head no.

Becky was a dedicated feminist who was very active in the

local radical women's group. She took great pride in her participation in the lesbian billboard bombing brigade. She didn't shave, wear makeup, or associate with men. I was the opposite. I thought our love could surpass all our differences, but we argued constantly. At one point she burst into tears over my friendship with two heterosexual men I had met in school. She couldn't understand why I had to be friends with those men. I told her they were my friends, just like anyone else—man, woman, gay, or straight. Becky had a very difficult time with this. She objected to my friendship with these guys simply because they were men. She had no logical explanation for it; it was something she "just felt." She wanted me to respect these feelings in her. I was disappointed and angry and told her that she had to respect my feelings and my rights too. After a big tear-filled fight, she finally relented and said I could bring them over, though she wouldn't be happy about it. When my friend Mark came over to make cookies with me, Becky said hi, then retreated to her room for the rest of the evening.

The differences between us didn't end there. Becky felt there were only certain ways two women should make love. In no way were we to do anything that might be regarded as an imitation of anything heterosexual. It felt so awful to be told that what I liked was wrong. I remember telling Becky I had done these things before and no one had ever said that I shouldn't. Sad, frustrated, and desperate, I took her to a bookstore and showed her in *The Joy of Lesbian Sex* the different kinds of lovemaking that were possible between women. The lesbian love bible said that what I liked was okay, so Becky relented.

One day I got Becky to join me at a party at a local bar with the women's rugby team I played for. I didn't like to drink, but I managed to have a great time dancing on tables that evening with some of the other players. Later, when we returned home, I remarked to Becky that I'd had a blast at the party. Becky turned to me and said very quietly that she was appalled by my behavior. I couldn't believe it. I hadn't been drinking, the team didn't get kicked out of the bar, and I'd had the time of my life, but instead of being happy and festive, my girlfriend was appalled and embarrassed. Suddenly I felt very sad, for I knew then that our relationship had reached a turning point: we were just too damn different.

Becky and I loved each other dearly, but I continually felt judged by her. I wanted her to accept me, but I saw myself conforming more and more in an effort to please her. Becky, in turn, was frustrated that I never acted the way she thought I should. It became more and more painful for us to remain together. Our differences seemed always to get in the way of our feelings. Loving each other just wasn't enough. After two years of this, we broke up. I felt we were still in love, but our differences, as they say, were irreconcilable. Becky left town. She said she had to be far away from me. I was furious that she moved away and sad because it seemed that I would never see her again. At her insistence, and through many, many phone calls and letters, we managed to work through a lot of our hurt and anger. This took about a year. I still loved Becky, but now I loved her as a friend. She said she felt the same way. When we got involved with other people, we were jealous of those replacement lovers. Becky told me she fantasized that when we grew old, we'd get back together. This made me feel good. It was nice to know she still cared so deeply about me.

With time, we developed a friendship that seemed better than what we'd had as lovers. Years before, Becky and I had thought we would be partners forever. Now, no longer lovers, we felt we still were partners. Becky had mellowed in her judgment toward me. She had the love and acceptance of her family, was establishing a successful career, and seemed happy. We lived in different states, but we saw each other two or three times a year. She met my friends, I met hers. We took vacations together at her family's cabin in Canada, took bike trips, went camping and skiing. Becky would drop everything to listen to me and provide encouragement and support. I'd had difficulties with my dissertation adviser, and she encouraged me to stick with it, backing me up when I "fired" my adviser and celebrating with me when I finished my dissertation. At other times, particularly when I was going through some difficult issues with my family, she supported me with the understanding that comes only from having known someone for a long time. Her guidance and kind words of assurance were a constant comfort to me. We were dedicated to one another; we knew each other's strengths and weaknesses. Becky defended anything I did. I did the same for her and told her if ever there was such a thing as unconditional love, I felt the two of us had it.

Time passed. Becky gave me a call one day and told me that she and her partner of six years were having problems. While I had suspected Becky was not totally happy with this woman, I was a bit surprised that their relationship was in trouble. She told me she had fallen for someone else. I asked her who it was. She paused, took a breath, and said his name was John. I was stunned. Somehow, though, I wasn't surprised. I guess I always suspected that Becky was bisexual. She had put so much effort into being a bona fide lesbian that I felt it could only have been because of something uncertain inside her. It was a good thing we were talking on the phone. I didn't know how to disguise the immediate feelings of outrage I'm sure were displayed all over my face. I wanted to confront her about the gross irony of her actions, but I felt I could do this later. Right now I was talking to someone I cared about who was in pain and felt obvious trepidation in revealing its source. I tried to stay calm and worked hard to listen to her. It wasn't easy.

Becky called me often to talk about her ongoing breakup, the difficult property settlement, the lawyers, the hurt, the anger. She mentioned little about John until the day she finally responded to my questioning by saying that she had fallen in love with him. I cared deeply for Becky, and I didn't mind her asking me for support through this divorce. But I couldn't stand her blatant disregard for the way she had treated me in regard to my male friends and the way, now that she had switched gears, she automatically expected me to do the same. It was also hard at first for me to accept the fact that my lesbian best friend was now with a man. But I had to keep rethinking things: we were close friends and had both been through a lot. I had to keep focused on another fact: she was still my partner and she just happened to be in love with someone who happened to be a man. That was the plain-and-simple of it. Nevertheless, I told her that I was taken aback that she was with a man and, for the simple reason of wanting things to stay the way they were, I would have much preferred it if she wasn't.

Several months later my girlfriend and I broke up, so Becky invited me to her house to spend some time away from home. I hadn't met John yet, and I was nervous about seeing him, but I figured that any man who was in love with a former lesbian had to be pretty cool.

Cool was exactly how he was with me. He never seemed to feel comfortable, didn't speak to me unless I asked him a question, and clearly gave the impression that he wanted as little as possible to do with my presence in his or Becky's life.

Things went from bad to worse when Becky and I cooked an elaborate dinner together and she had to ask John to set the table. I don't know why this set me off—maybe because I had paid attention only to the "male" side of him. The part that didn't cook or help out in the kitchen, the part that watched sports on TV and played in the local hockey club. I guess I had expected a woman in a man's body, or at least an "Alan Alda NOW" kind of feminist. After all, I thought, who else could be the partner of a woman who was so feminist, so political, so previously anti-male? When I saw, from outward appearances, that John was quite different from my expectations, anger toward Becky began to surface. I told her that it was a shame that John had to be asked to set the table. She defended him, which only made me madder. He left the room in a huff because I had "reduced him to nothing more than a person of the male species." I told Becky it was a little hard for me to be nonreductive with a person who had only grunted in my direction the entire time I had been there. And furthermore, I continued, it was a little hard to be supportive of a friend who had been so intolerant of my own friendships with men years before.

Her reply was succinct: "People change."

Eventually I got over my difficulties with this new love. Becky was in love with John, and there was nothing I could do, even if I wanted to, to change that reality. On a trip she and I took together to Lake Tahoe, I told her I had accepted John as part of her life. I also said that it was important to me that we remain friends, since John wasn't speaking to me and was obviously uncomfortable whenever I visited. Becky didn't want to talk much about John's feelings. She only said that he had been hurt because he felt I had regarded him simply as a "man" and not as a person. I told her that was my first reaction, but the real reason was my anger toward her for the way she had treated me previously. Becky seemed to understand and agree with my position, but she still rationalized John's responses. She spoke in an expressionless, "just the facts, ma'am" manner, which frightened me. I wanted her to do something, say something to John about his ill-founded feelings toward me. The fact that she seemed to accept all of this without contesting anything, without confronting him, made me feel that she no longer felt the same about me. I started to cry. I told Becky our relationship was in jeopardy and that I didn't want to lose her. I said that we had been loyal to each other, that I loved her as my friend, and that I wanted to be in her life. I hoped she wanted the same. Although she was characteristically stoic, she too began to cry and said that she did feel the same way. I felt optimistic that we would be able to work things out.

I didn't see Becky again until the following summer, when we went camping together. I thought it was odd that she had agreed to spend a long weekend away from her home, away from John. Though the weather was chilly, our camping trip went well and we had a good time. Becky managed to talk me into sea kayaking, which she enjoyed tremendously, while I counted the strokes back to our campsite and a cup of hot chocolate. When I asked her about John, she said the summer was the height of his work period and he was busy.

I saw her once again, that fall. I had to do some work in the area, so I went up to her place for a long weekend with a woman I was dating. I assumed that John had gotten over his ill feelings toward me—after all, it had been well over a year since our initial encounter—and I was happily expecting a pleasant visit. Unfortunately, that wasn't to be. John spoke to me only when I asked him a direct question. He didn't look at me when I addressed him or when he was talking to the group in general. I thought it was ridiculous of him to hold a grudge for so long, so I asked Becky what was wrong. She didn't want to talk about it. She said that John was still having some difficulty dealing with our initial encounter a year and a half ago. I said that was a long time to be angry over an issue that wasn't even about him. He still thought I was "anti-male," Becky responded. I breathed a long sigh. "For crying out loud, Becky," I told her. "You know I don't feel that way." I wondered if the two of them had ever really spoken about this subject and, if so, what Becky had said. I told her I thought it was unfortunate that John still had the same feelings about me.

Becky and I spoke throughout the fall and winter. She had always wanted to have a child, even when we were together. John was against it. According to Becky, he was afraid of commitments. They underwent counseling, where a deadline for his final decision was to be set. I asked Becky if she was going to marry John. She said she would if they were to have a child. The day of the deadline arrived: in tears, John told Becky that he would go along with her having a baby. Becky was happy. I was worried, because according to Becky, the tears John had shed were not tears of joy. And no wonder—Becky's intention was to have a baby with or without him.

In the meantime I had bought a house, and Becky was anxious to see it. She called me one morning to tell me she was coming to the Bay Area to visit me. I asked her if John was coming too, since I always made a point of including him in my invitations. She said no, he was busy with work. She also told me, without skipping a beat, that she thought it best if our visits all happened at my place instead of hers from now on. I thought I had misheard her, so I asked her to clarify what she meant. She repeated it. For some reason it still wasn't sinking in. I asked her if she meant that I wasn't to come to her house anymore. She said "Yeah, kind of like that." Then she chuckled softly.

I couldn't believe that I no longer was allowed into the home of a person I had considered my friend and partner of eleven years, and that she could be so cavalier about telling me so. Becky changed the subject. She talked about the things we were going to do when she arrived for her visit. I was hurt. I reacted as I had as a kid: whenever something terrible happened to me, I simply shut off my feelings from any more hurt. I can't even remember what else she said to me. I replied with an "okay" to everything she said. I hung up, stunned. For two days I stewed over Becky's announcement. I tried to figure out why she had laid down this rule. I knew there was a connection to John, but what was it? I knew he was uncomfortable with me, but I never thought he would tell her to keep me out of the house. I got more and more angry. I decided it would be best to talk to Becky and tell her my feelings.

I called her back on a Monday morning. I started by telling her that I cared about her a great deal and that I thought a lot about what she'd said to me. I wanted her to know how surprised I was that I was no longer welcome in her house. I had always felt that she had the integrity to stand by her feelings, no matter how difficult. But here she was, casting me off in a clear indication of disrespect for me and for our friendship. It seemed so ironic that a man, her man, would come between us. I also said that I couldn't believe how cavalier she had been when she told me this. She apologized for her casual tone and said she "was just trying not to make a big deal about it." I asked her if all this had happened because of John's feelings toward me, and she said, "Pretty much, that's what it is." I was outraged. We've been friends for over eleven years, I continued. Didn't that mean anything to her? I thought we were partners, I told her in tears. Her voice was like cold steel. "These things take time," was all she said. I replied that I didn't want her to come visit me. "How could our friendship matter, how could *I* matter when I'm no longer welcome in your house?"

Suddenly I realized the futility of it all. "I'm very hurt and sad," I said slowly, softly. In the same steely tone of voice she told me she was sorry I felt this way, but if that was how I felt, then she would go along with it and not come to visit. I said I loved her and that I too was sorry it had come down to this. She said okay and good-bye without any emotion that I could detect, except anger. We hung up. That was the last time we spoke.

After a week or so I wrote her a card telling her that I hoped we could work this out. I didn't hear from her. Four months passed. Her birthday was in November, and I sent her a card to let her know I was thinking of her and still hoping we could speak to each other. Two months later I finally got a card from her. She said it had taken that long for her anger to quell enough for her to write me. Essentially, she felt that this was a problem between me and John, that she was caught in the middle, and that she didn't like being placed in this position. She said he still harbored old feelings of distrust toward me, and it didn't seem likely that he would ever get over them. This was just something I would have to deal with. After that, she went on as if nothing had ever happened between us; she spoke about work and family. There were no words of sorrow, no expressions of remorse or regret. Becky had made a decision: if we were to remain friends, we would have to accommodate John's wishes and needs. This, essentially, was the end of the discussion.

I had been losing sleep, thinking every day about the loss of Becky's friendship. I knew I had to make one more attempt to reconcile with her. I did not call her. I feared another angry argument fueled by betrayal and hurt. I wanted to write while I was calm and clearheaded. I wrote once again telling her that I was sad, still hurt, and mad that she placed greater value on John's feelings than on our friendship of eleven years. I also told her that I thought it would make things easier for her relationship with John to have me out of the picture, since her friendship with me brought up all the insecurities he had about Becky and her lesbian past. What had happened to that friend who used to stand up for the things she believed in? I said it was too easy to place the blame on a conflict between me and John. Becky wanted no part of that conflict, no responsibility. "You can't just walk away from this," I wrote her, "or can you?" I told her that I still hoped we could work this out and that I loved her as my friend. Then I mailed the letter.

It has been over a year since I wrote that letter to Becky. I haven't heard a word from her. I don't know if she got married and had the baby she always dreamed of. I don't know if her father and her sweet grandma are still with us. I don't know what her nephew is learning in school or what's happening with her sisters and brother. I don't know anything anymore about Becky or a family I once adopted as mine. I've accepted the fact that Becky does not want me in her life. What's really hard to accept is why.

The Kick Inside

by Martha Southgate

When Rebecca kicked me in the stomach, it wasn't anything like what I was used to. I'd been kicked before, but this was different.

Before I started training, all I knew about karate came from Bruce Lee movies and from Wesley, this fool I lived with who had some nunchakus, those rubber things with a chain that you can throw at people. He thought he was real macho with those. After we'd been together for a while, he started talking about using them on me. That was when I threw his ass out of my life. I don't put up with that kind of treatment anymore. Not since I left home.

The good thing about it, though, was that I started thinking about taking karate myself. That plus I have this friend, Ruth, who used to take classes at this all-women dojo where I now train. She's real into women—she's the first black woman I ever met who calls herself a feminist—and she's got me almost convinced. Her life is so together. If hanging around a lot of women is a way to get to where she's at, I'll try it. I'm willing to try anything at this point.

Anyway, Ruth was always telling me how important it is to be around a lot of female energy, and she invited me to come and watch a karate class one day. I'd never seen anything like it. Here were all these women, all different, sparring with each other and laughing, doing these beautiful forms called kata, looking so strong and sure of themselves. I was a little skeptical when I first walked in because almost all of the women were white and a lot of them were kind of butch-looking—lots of hairy legs—but by the time the class ended, I couldn't deny the power in that room. I told Ruth that day that I wanted to start training. She just smiled and said, "I thought you would."

Karla, my therapist, was all for me starting, too. She thought it would be a good way for me to "let go of some hostility in a physical way." I have to admit that I like all the yelling we do in class. I feel as if I've left my skinny-legged body behind, as if I'm all roaring voice and dark-eyed rage. And whenever we kick at the heavy bags or at the air, my father's face floats in front of me like one of those balloons on a string.

When Rebecca kicked me, I was sparring with her. I had just tried to throw a couple of punches, and before I knew it, she had flashed out this round kick and hit me dead in the stomach. My first impulse was to do what I had always done with my dad—get away first and plot my revenge later. I backed away fast, keeping my guard up. I looked at her small pale face and thought about how I would hit her if she kicked me again. I must have looked angry or hurt, because she stopped right away and asked if I was all right. She looked really worried.

I rubbed my eyes and took a deep breath, trying to stop the buzzing in my head. "Yeah, yeah, I'm fine. You just caught me by surprise."

"Still, I'm really sorry, Pam. You've only been training what, a year? I should have been more careful." Then she touched me on the shoulder and smiled. "You're sure you're okay?"

That touch was so different from what I'd expected. I was used to one kick following another, and then another after that. But Rebecca was really concerned that she'd hurt me. I rubbed my stomach for a second. "Yeah, I'm fine. Just let me catch my breath."

Afterward in the dressing room, she apologized again. Then she looked at me for a minute longer and asked, "Are you doing anything after class? Do you want to go get some lunch somewhere?"

I was surprised. Nobody at the school had ever asked me to do anything with them. Karla said that might have been because I was afraid to give them a chance to get to know me. I just figured I had nothing in common with these white girls.

"You really don't have to take me to lunch because you kicked me, you know," I said.

"That's not why I want to take you to lunch."

All right then, I thought, let's just see what she does want. "Okay."

We walked to this little coffee shop near the dojo. It's in this mostly white yuppie neighborhood. There were all these happy-looking couples out on the street, with babies in those blue backpacks and in expensive-looking strollers. I felt the same way I feel at work, as if I wasn't really a part of things, as if some kind of invisible shield had cut me off from the rest of the world.

Rebecca had her head bent, and I kept sneaking little looks at her. She's got short dark brown hair and blue eyes. Really perfect skin, that Irish skin that doesn't have any pores. Like a model's.

After we sat down, it was a little easier to talk. I could still feel the tender place where she'd kicked me. I didn't touch it, but I could feel it just above my belt buckle. It felt like it was going to bruise. She asked why I'd started taking karate.

"I never really thought about it a lot before. I guess I wanted to feel like I could beat up anybody who messed with me. I never thought I'd end up staying this long."

"I'm glad you like it," she said. She hesitated for a minute. "Sometimes I think it's harder for black women to stay at the school because there are so few of them in the classes. I think it's great that you've stayed."

"Did you want to have lunch with me to congratulate me for being black?"

She turned red and looked as if she didn't know what to say. "I . . . didn't want to sound stupid or patronizing. I . . ."

I let her stew for a minute. Sometimes you just need to pull these white girls up short. I've met so many well-intentioned ones—lots of times, they're the worst. But I wasn't really angry with her. And as I looked at her face, I realized I'd been messing with her for no good reason. Maybe this was what Karla meant when she said I pushed people away.

So I smiled and said, "Don't worry. I'm just giving you a hard time. I'm glad that you at least think about this stuff. A lot of people don't."

She smiled back and said, "Don't compliment me when I don't deserve it. I didn't mean to put you on the spot. Why don't we just start this conversation over?"

So we did. She told me how she'd started doing karate when she saw some women from the school at a rally. She works for a book publisher as an assistant. She actually likes her job. I can't imagine what that would be like. I'm a word processor. I hate it, but I don't know what else to do right now. I got my GED last year—I did really well on it, too—and I've taken a couple of classes at Brooklyn College, but it's going slow. Ruth's my only friend in the city, but since she got married and had a little boy, I don't see her as much as I used to.

It turned out to be nice, talking to Rebecca. She was really easy to talk to. Funny and smart. She started telling me this story about a trip she took out west, and then she said "My old girlfriend and I always wanted to do it again sometime, but then we broke up, so we weren't able to. Maybe I'll get to go out west another time, though. With somebody else."

When she said that, it was like all the other noise in the restaurant stopped. I couldn't even hear the babies crying anymore. Her old girlfriend? Oh, man.

She kept talking, but her voice sounded real far away. A white girl and a lesbian. I'd never had a long conversation like this with a lesbian before. I'd been on my own for ten years, since I was seventeen, so I'd met a few, and I knew that a lot of the women at the school were gay. But I hadn't tried to talk to any of them. I had kind of steered clear of them because all the lesbians I'd ever known were pretty sad cases. Always fighting with their girlfriends.

Rebecca was different. She seemed real regular. She just talked to me like another person, not like a cultural experience. And she seemed honestly interested in what I had to say about things. But a lesbian. Wow. I always thought that didn't bother me that much, but now . . . I did feel a little funny. I hoped she couldn't tell.

We finished and paid. When we were outside, she looked at me that same direct way again and said, "I had a really good time. We should do this again sometime."

I was thinking that she wasn't like anyone else I knew. But all I said was "I'd really like that."

I was restless all that evening. I rented a movie but couldn't pay attention. I kept thinking about Rebecca. Knowing she was gay made me feel weird, but not bad. I never thought it was such a big goddamn deal. The worst thing you could call somebody back in Detroit was a dyke. I used to laugh along—I was afraid not to—but in my head I never hated lesbians. At least they had someone to love.

I thought about how unafraid Rebecca seemed. There weren't any secret messages hidden in the way she talked. She didn't seem to want to take anything away from me. She was just there, solid, not apologizing, not angry. I wanted to find that kind of confidence in myself, to take it in from her. I used to think that I didn't want anyone around me, that I could do everything by myself. Life was safer that way. But after I met Ruth and I started going to see Karla, things began to change. I don't know. It's scary, feeling things again. But I couldn't stop thinking about the way Rebecca had been so concerned about hurting me, and about the way her hands moved when she talked, like small white birds.

The next morning when I got up, I knew I had dreamed about her. Sometimes you wake up and you can't remember what the dream was, you just know who was in it and it's like they've touched you. Like you know them better somehow. I felt as if I'd had my hands in her hair all night.

When I was in tenth grade and my father was beating me up almost every day, I had this friend, Sandra. I have one picture of us. We're both looking at the camera with our teeth showing in imitation smiles, our eyes flat and shiny with rage. Sandra was short and dark-skinned and fat and she wore thick glasses. People called us Fatty and Skinny after that kids' movie they used to show on Saturday afternoons. I think we got to be friends because we both loved to read but we didn't like school. We just wanted to read what we felt like. I remember she especially liked James Baldwin and that guy who wrote *The Postman Always Rings Twice,* James Cain. She turned me on to both of them. Her mother was drunk all the time, so Sandra was pretty much free to do what she wanted when she wanted.

We would sit behind the school, smoking cigarettes and plotting how we were going to get the hell out of Detroit and never look back. One time when we were hiding out there after an especially bad night with my father, I started crying real hard. I couldn't help it, I didn't know how much more I could take.

Sandra held me while I cried. Then without either of us knowing how it happened, she started kissing me all over my face, brushing the tears away. When we broke apart, our whole friendship was ruined. Sandra and I couldn't even look at each other. We stopped talking without even planning it. I met Kenny within a month and slept with him within a month after that.

I hadn't thought about Sandra in eight years. But ever since I talked to Rebecca all these kinds of things kept coming back to me. Stuff I thought I'd put behind me, stuff I hadn't even told Karla or Ruth. It was like something inside me got kicked loose that day. Everything began to rattle after that.

Weeks went by when I couldn't concentrate at work. I typed stuff and didn't even know what I was typing. I went to class, I talked to the same few people I always did at work, asking what they had done over the weekend, and what about those Mets? I ate lunch outside at one of those little office plazas by myself, like I always did, but I kept thinking about Rebecca. I wished I could have lunch with her again. I saw her in class and we talked a little bit, but we didn't go out again. Because it was summer my therapist was on vacation, so she couldn't pick this thing apart. I didn't really want her to, anyway. Sometimes I hate telling her things. Ruth was on vacation with her husband and their son, so I couldn't talk to her either—not that I would have told her. What was to tell, anyway?

One Saturday about a month after I had lunch with Rebecca, I had a really hard time figuring out what to wear to karate class. I tried on three different T-shirts and wore my favorite shorts. I felt a little ridiculous but I couldn't stop myself. I knew that it had something to do with Rebecca, but I didn't know what.

The dressing room was crowded, as it always is. People were yelling back and forth, as they always are. Rebecca wasn't there, though. And she still wasn't there when we got called onto the floor.

It was really hot that day, so almost everybody was training in just a T-shirt or a tank top, not their *gi*. We were doing the warm-up exercises when Rebecca came in. You know how you can see someone and everything is different all of a sudden? There's nothing gradual about it. You're just going along, minding your own business, and then, pow, there's this person that you have to be with and you didn't even know it? That's how I felt when Rebecca came onto the floor in a tank top.

At the sight of her arms, I thought I was going to start crying. I'd never seen anything so beautiful. I could no longer ignore what I was feeling. I didn't want to. In karate they're always telling us to follow our own path. And I felt that the sight of her arms, her face, the soft brown of her hair, that dream I had, were all lying in front of me like a dark road I had to travel, even though I didn't know where it would take me.

I went through the rest of class in a blur. After class, I went right up to her.

"Hi, Rebecca. How are you?"

"I'm good, Pam. How are you?"

"Good." I stopped for a minute. I thought of when I was little and things were still okay at home, the way my mother used to touch me on the back before I had to do anything I was afraid of. She said it would bring me luck.

"Listen," I said, "I hope you don't think this is weird but . . . are you free tonight? I'd like to have dinner with you or something."

"I'd love that," she said. "Where do you want to go?"

We went to this nice place in Fort Greene for dinner. It's near where I live and it's not too expensive. They'll let you sit as long as you want. All afternoon, ever since I'd asked her, I'd felt this quiet hum in the back of my head, like an organ note in an empty church. It made it hard to hear what she was saying, made each feature separate and distinct. Eyes so blue you could fall into them. Hair thick, dark brown, shiny. Strong-looking hands that she kept gesturing with. I could only imagine them touching me, taking her fingers in my mouth. What was she saying? She told me how she'd grown up in Kansas, how she had moved to New York five years ago when she was twenty-one. How her parents were upset when she told them she was gay but then they came around after a few years.

She asked me how long I'd been in New York. Seven years, I told her, since I was twenty. She looked at me the same way she did when we had lunch, like she was really seeing me, like I mattered. I felt like laying my head right down on the table in front of her. I could barely breathe. But I could feel the image of that bruise on my stomach. So I had to tell her.

I told her about my father, how he used to beat me up. After my mother died when I was eight, something happened to him. It started slow, just an occasional slap. I would almost think it was a regular spanking. But then it got worse and worse. He'd hit me in the face, on my back, call me all kinds of horrible names. I never knew what would set him off. I put up with it, hid the bruises once I got old enough. It was never so bad that my teachers noticed. He seemed to know that if he hit my face too hard he'd risk being caught. I managed to survive until I was sixteen and could leave school. But I learned how to hide things. I learned how to hide everything.

I never fought back against my father until one night when I was seventeen. I came home from my job at a 7-Eleven one night and found him going after my sister. I didn't even think. Everything went black, then red, in front of my eyes. He was hitting her and hitting her, and somehow—I don't remember how—I got to the kitchen drawer. Got it open. Pulled a knife out. Screamed at him, "Get your fucking hands off her. Get them off her now!" She was only eleven, and she hung on to my leg so tight I could feel a pulse there; I don't know if it was hers or mine. I remember the way he looked at me, like I was something he'd found on the bottom of his shoe, his eyes all red. And then he just turned and walked out.

My sister and I left Detroit that same night. I spent all the money I had earned from my 7-Eleven job to buy our bus tickets. My sister lives with my aunt, my mother's sister, in Atlanta now. I can only afford to go down to see her a couple of times a year. She's doing pretty well. I worked there for a while, but then I followed this guy Wesley to New York. He turned out to be a user, not a savior. I would have left New York, but I met Ruth and she helped me get into this sliding-fee counseling service. I'm trying to make my life into something I want. But it's hard.

My heart pounded the whole time I told Rebecca this. But I never thought about stopping. I wanted her to know everything.

Rebecca just looked at me when I stopped talking. Her eyes were very bright. "Your life then must have been awful."

I brushed at my eyes with the back of my hand. "Yeah."

She looked at her plate for a minute. Then she looked up and spoke abruptly. "Pam. I know you're . . . well, you've never been with a woman before, but I've got to tell you. You are so beautiful. I don't want to scare you, but I had to say it. I'm . . . well, you know . . . I want you very much."

She looked scared while she was saying all this, but she never turned her eyes away. It was like she was kissing me. I wanted to touch her so bad that felt my heart contract under my ribs.

"Let's get out of here," I said.

We walked back to my apartment, our arms almost touching. There was nothing to say. We went inside and leaned up against the door, still not talking. Then my hands were in her hair and she was kissing me for real. It was like I'd never felt any pain in my life, only her hands on my back, her mouth on mine. I felt stunned, the same way I felt when she kicked me in the stomach. But this time it was a good surprise. Like the last Christmas my mother was alive. I remember running down the stairs, with that cold air on my bare feet, my mom and dad smiling at us. I felt that there were all these wonderful things ahead, that nothing bad would ever happen to any of us.

All of a sudden it was as if I'd stepped outside my body for a second. I saw myself in my doorway kissing another woman. And I froze. Just like that time with Sandra.

My eyes stung as Rebecca pulled away from me. "This isn't all right, is it?" she said softly.

My voice wouldn't come out right. "I don't know. I want to. I do. But I'm so scared."

She ran her hand gently across my face, my hair, and smiled a little. "Yeah. I know." She kissed me on the forehead. "I'm going to go now. But I gave you my number. Call me. Please."

I closed the door behind her and leaned against it for a minute or two. Then I slid down to the floor, bawling. I hadn't done that in years. I was so tired of being afraid. I was so tired of keeping it all in. I just couldn't do it anymore. After a while, I stopped crying and went to splash water on my face. I dried my hands and, without thinking, reached into my pocket. The little piece of paper Rebecca had written her number on was still there. I pulled it out and ran my fingers over the graceful writing, thinking about how much Sandra and I had loved each other and how we had thrown it away; what a stupid waste that was. Then I went and picked up the phone.

3

Curiosity, Desire, and Sex

What Is It About Straight Women?

by Susie Bright

FALL 1985

Oh, no, not us. Why would a lesbian be attracted to a straight woman? You don't need her anxiety, you don't need her husband, and the charm of her naïveté wears off real fast. She'll use you—but good. The Lesbian Nation doesn't need this grief.

Nevertheless what is it about straight women? They're not everyone's kink, but the straight-gay attraction is definitely one of the most popular and enduring games in town.

The appeal of straight women is buried in mystique. Lesbians who are persistently attracted to straight women are reluctant to spell out what is so attractive to them about heterosexuals.

"Straight, my ass!" says one seasoned Lady Lover. "I've pulled more bitches out of straight bars than I ever did out of girls' bars."

"They always come on to me," another Lady Lover insists. "It's classic. She'll say, 'I never knew it could be like this . . .'"

"And then leave you," chimes in another veteran. "You can always count on that."

Let's lift the swirling mist of troubled emotions that has clouded the real issue behind affairs with straight women. The truth is, straight girls can be a hot fantasy or an enduring sexual preference. We know who *they* are, but what is it about us that prompts the attraction? What kind of lesbian is a lover of straight women?

The typical Lady Lover is a Doubting Thomas. She doesn't label her lovers one way or the other. She claims to be nonjudgmental. Despite her last seventeen consecutive affairs with straight women, she denies that their heterosexuality has anything to do with the attraction.

Well, if Ms. Thomas is too chicken to judge, we will. Her straight lovers' heterosexuality has quite a bit to do with that "uncanny" appeal. Bringing out a woman, without any doubt, is a very intoxicating experience.

There are other species in the ranks of Lady Lovers Anonymous. One is the Separatist. Every dyke who scorns heterosexual women was once, or still is, in love with them. Feminism provided a convenient set of politics with which you could dismiss straight women right out of your life. But for all the global rhetoric, the bottom line remains: She rejected you, possibly for a prick, and rejection is exquisitely bitter. You blame yourself for believing you could change her, and you'll never be fooled again. Until next time . . .

The real power, the real glory in store for the dedicated Lady Lover is not all this sobbing into pillows and gnashing one's teeth. The power is to accept the Straight Woman for what she is: the object of your lust. A fantasy you can masturbate over. A fling at the office, a seasonal romance. It can even be a scene you play out with a lesbian lover: "You'll be the rich straight lady leaning over the avocados in the gourmet section of Safeway, and I'll be the friendly lesbian who stares down your blouse."

In order to "come out" as a Lady Lover, it helps to articulate just what is attractive about straight women. Let's go over the basics:

1. There is nothing like a good challenge. *They* are supposedly unattainable, but *you* know your mouth and hands could make the difference. We Ladykillers experience sexual triumphs.
2. Straight women take their femininity for granted. This is particularly fascinating to lesbian butches. *They* are so utterly cool and unquashable in their womanhood, never troubled by a tomboy image or a queer's insecurity. Any Liz Taylor movie will prove this.
3. We see ourselves on a Mission of Love, as initiators of virgins. We are delighted by their wonder and eagerness. We have so much to teach, and their appetites are so enormous.
4. Straight women live outside of gay culture. Obvious, yes, but so often this is the motivation. Many a disgruntled bar dyke or burned-out lesbian activist is drawn to the woman who doesn't have a damn thing to do with us: our cliques, our habits, our hang-ups. Straight women *do* have their own hang-ups, which we don't notice at first in all the excitement.

Never let it be said that straight women are all alike. There are definite types, which in our phobia of labeling, we have never had the good sense to name.

Butch-femme terminology comes in handy here. Ordinarily, butch-femme is a description reserved for gay territory, but the same naming of style is helpful and perhaps appropriate to describe our heterosexual turn-ons.

For example, "The Doctor's Wife" is a Femme Straight Woman. She seems to have a lot of time and a lot of jewelry on her hands. She hides her vibrator from her husband, and she nearly died when you put your whole hand inside her. She's very thin, very clean, and she screams when she comes.

"The Roots Woman" is the Butch Straight Woman. She is surrounded by children, animals, and useless men. She's as tough as nails, you feel like making a documentary of her life, and her chest is heaven. She's never come before. You broke through her cynicism, built from three alcoholic husbands. The two of you get it on in the back of the station wagon at a drive-in while the kids are outside fighting over candy.

The list goes on. Class, race, age, and a softball team can each add endless variations. Once you have identified your straight woman fantasy as part of your erotic identity, you can truly begin to enjoy yourself. Think of her as you would any other fantasy. Do you really want to act out this fantasy, or would it lose something in the translation? Probably some experimentation will be necessary.

If straight women are definitely your sexual preference, then start appreciating the sex, instead of complaining about the limitations of the relationship. If what you love is bringing them out, why stick around to become bored and frustrated by the aftermath? If you want a vacation from the gay community, don't expect *her* to follow *our* rules.

Straight women are a lot more savvy about why they're attracted to us. We know how to kiss. We perform oral sex as a matter of course. We fuck like angels—and they never knew dry humping could be so much fun. Lesbianism is the delight of endless foreplay, foreplay with orgasms. Our skin is soft, just like theirs.

Now, you know, some straight ladies will fool you and end up becoming lesbians after all. They'll start making love back to you and come up with all kinds of little tricks that will make your clit jump up and wonder where the time went. All of a sudden your precious, innocent straight lady will be gone. You'll find yourself instead with a real live Sapphic Wonder.

At this point you might want to take her aside and confess that, if the truth be known, you used to be sort of a straight woman, too.

A Closet of One's Own : On Not Becoming a Lesbian

by Daphne Merkin

Although I have preferred the company of my own sex to that of men for as far back as I can remember, I've never had a lesbian experience. I've never been close to a gay woman, either, though for a while I carried on a bantering friendship with a self-described "dyke" I met during a brief hospitalization for depression. This woman was great fun to be around; she was also very overweight and sported the kind of G.I. Joe haircut I associated with women who put their tongues in each other's mouths when they kissed instead of politely brushing the cheek. Toward the end of my hospital stay the two of us regularly signed up for passes to go out to dinner; usually we went for sushi in the next town over, but one evening we planned to have dinner at an elegant inn about an hour's drive away. On the afternoon of that evening, flowers were delivered to me; they were from my friend, and I suddenly realized that she might be reading more into our outings than I intended. That night at the inn, over candles and glistening tableware, I felt other people's glances on us. I wasn't sure whether it was because my companion was not only obese but given to an excessive style in general, or whether everyone suspected us of being lovers. I felt palpably uncomfortable, and as the evening wore on, our conversation grew ever more stiff. Over dessert I decided to confront the situation directly; I explained that I had greatly appreciated the flowers but was a bit taken aback by the sheer romanticness of her gesture. She understood what I meant, and the affair was over before it had begun.

I find it striking that I don't count any lesbians among my good friends, and even more surprising that over the years I've met only a handful of women who have openly acknowledged their gayness—as opposed to having this aspect of themselves bruited about as gossip or speculation. Even so, somewhere along the way, in spite of my limited exposure, I've sensed that gay women are drawn to me. I suppose it's because I lead with my brain—something most men still react to with undisguised alarm—and because I exude the sort of attentiveness toward other women that most women save for men.

Still, I have trouble to this day imagining what it would be like to have a woman's tongue in my mouth, much less in my more intimate parts. When I say I have trouble, I mean that I literally balk at the picture: my mind closes down, resists further exploration. Perhaps this makes me a card-carrying heterosexual; more likely, it signifies nothing more than that I am a culturally conditioned woman who has tailored her erotic fantasies to fit the expectations of her time and place.

I was twelve or thereabouts when I first came upon the word "lesbian" ascribed to some misfortunate female or other; it caught my eye, like a bright red ball tossed up into the air. I can't remember any longer whether it was used to describe a character in one of the novels I was ceaselessly burying myself in or if it was said of someone I knew in real life. I also can't recall what, exactly, I thought being a lesbian was all about. I knew it had to do with favoring the company of women over men, but beyond that I don't think I envisioned much of anything. What I do remember, clear as can be, is the ping of recognition that accompanied my discovery of the term: I immediately decided that this word—this dark and elusive *she* known as a "lesbian"—and I belonged together. I was, in fact, so convinced, and so terrified, of what I now deemed to be my linguistically determined fate that I immediately tried to eject it from my physical being. The thing to do, I decided, with a child's cruel instinct for exposure, was to hang my interior destiny out to air in the bracing atmosphere of the heterosexual world I inhabited: like a Sapphic Hester Prynne, I would wear my perverted identity emblazoned on my chest, the better to be cured of it.

I began by announcing to my senior counselor at the Orthodox Jewish summer camp I went to that I feared I wished to sleep next to my mother more than was ordinary. Just in case this innocent teenager in knee-knockers didn't get the message, I went on to spill the sordid beans: I feared, I said, that I was—and then I used the word aloud for the first time—a *lesbian*. Of course, what was really askew in my home life had less to do with any shameful libidinal yearnings toward my mother than with my wish to be closer to her than she allowed me to be. (As for my father, I had given up on him early on; he was as distant as the sky, and as impervious.) But I was a writerly young girl, and I wanted to keep my audience interested. To this end I leaped over the more obvious heartrending presentations of my childhood sorrows and landed on a sophisticated off-center version. Who would care if I was desperately homesick at camp for a mother I was desperately homesick for even when I was at home? Who would understand, even if I could have put it this way? I found it more acceptable to describe my longing for an unavailable mother as something tainted, even unnatural—as something wrong with *me*. The perception that there might be something wrong with my *parents* would come much later; in the meantime I blamed myself for my mother's inadequacies. I particularly blamed myself for resenting the fact that she locked her bedroom door at night, so that even as a small child I had been unable to go in to her for reassurance or hugs when I woke up from a bad dream or couldn't fall asleep. (Not one to take such inaccessibility lightly, I developed full-blown insomnia by the age of eight, but that's another story.)

The counselor was a sweet and earnest type, with a more than ordinary commitment to the Judaic principles on which the camp was founded. She took my confession to heart and immediately called my mother, who reassured this concerned messenger that my sudden interest in lesbianism was based on nothing more than something I'd been reading. And thus order was quickly restored: I learned how to wrap my hair around a juice can in order to make it as straight as a stick, and I continued to worry that my breasts were too big and my legs too thin whenever I took part in the endless dance- and song-fests the camp specialized in. Underneath it all I continued to pine for my mother, for her now-you-see-it, now-you-don't presence without which I floundered. Underneath it all, I felt bewildered by my bunkmates' consuming interest in the pimply, graceless boys on the other side of the camp, most of whom were idiots as far as I was concerned. What were boys to me and what was I to boys, I wondered, that I should give them the automatic edge over my girl-friends?

I wasn't completely immune to the opposite sex, however. That same summer I developed a crush on the camp's maintenance man. It helped that at an ancient nineteen or twenty, he was some years older than the boys my friends primped for, no longer a man-in-formation but a full-fledged man. His job, menial and smelly, also gave him a masculine glamour in my eyes, especially when compared with the goody-goody boys my own age who split their day between studying Torah and Talmud in the morning and swimming and playing tennis or baseball in the afternoon. Then, too, David F. was my idea of sexy—which is to say that he had a thin, withholding mouth and thereby suggested the essence of my mother's personality in male form. He gave me my first French kiss, or at least he tried; I screamed midway through it and scared him off. I told some of the other girls about it, and eventually my counselor heard about it. I was relieved when she came to me, full of concern about my disregard for the laws of *negiyah,* which limit physical contact between males and females who aren't married to one another. I was more than relieved, actually. I was triumphant that one identity had ousted the other: I had gone from being a potential lesbian to being a potential hussy, the genuine heterosexual article. Whatever lingering doubts I had were pushed aside. So what if I hadn't really liked the feel of David F.'s tongue, slimy and intrusive, inside my mouth? Would I have liked it any better if it had been the tongue of a girl?

I suppose somewhere along the way, however anxiety-ridden the issue of sexuality may be—as opposed to the greater chromosomal clarity of gender, of being born indisputably male or female—one reaches an intuitive decision, honors some impulses more than others. In the end, it may come down to no more than the inclination, in spite of some inner waffling, to throw one's behavioral weight behind certain norms. In the years that have passed since my blurted confession of lesbianism to my camp counselor, I have married and become a mother. These are things I wanted to do, although marriage came much harder to me than motherhood. I still look upon all men with a degree of suspicion I do not generally feel toward women, and I still feel that even men with developed sensibilities tend to be more obtuse than most women. But there is the undeniable fact that men arouse me physically—*some* men, that is, men with subtle, slightly feminine turns of mind, although I have also been captivated by men who strut like the proverbial rooster and who are not the least bit interested in what I am thinking or feeling. Women, although they generally tend to irritate me less than men, do not, to the best of my self-awareness, sexually excite me. I have sometimes thought that, given my psychological makeup, it would be easier all around if they did. . . .

As I have gotten older and observed the subject of lesbianism (as distinct from the issue of gay pride, which for the longest time translated into gay *male* pride) gain greater visibility, I note with curiosity that there still appears to be something innately dreary about the reflected image of gay women—a couple of singers (Melissa Etheridge, k.d. lang, and who knows about Madonna), a trendy bar scene, and a handful of glamorous "lipstick lesbians" notwithstanding. To feel this way is undoubtedly to date myself or to suggest some incriminating resistance on my part, for surely the lesbian image has been overhauled and polished to a flattering sheen since *The Children's Hour* was the operative cultural reference, with Shirley MacLaine in her Mamie Eisenhower bangs yearning silently for the boyishly lovely Audrey Hepburn.

So let me put it another way by saying that, even in the shadow of AIDS, men loving men has an authenticity—a quality of being on to something valid that the straight world has overlooked in all its heterosexual zeal—that women loving women doesn't have, at least for me. When I think of two men together, I have a sense of what they're about: the ineluctable force of it, the sidestepping of the many restrictive rules by which our thinking about sexually ordained behavior—what is allowably masculine or feminine—is governed. But when I think of two women together, I think of it as the default position; immediately there comes over me a feeling of the compensatory—of dildos and harnesses and other role-playing apparatus, mental as well as physical.

Somewhere in this assessment, of course, floats a sadder, more insidious piece of reality, having to do with the way women continue to be perceived by society at large and how we in turn assess one another. Contaminated by a cultural outlook that casts my own kind as somehow deficient or lesser than, I can see only that if straight women are not as powerful as straight men, gay women seem to be huddled together in some shabby third-class lounge. (Gay men, on the other hand, often appear to have invented a republic of their own, like that of ancient Greece, where women and straight men have ceased to be of any importance.) Some of this perception is based on the sense I have that the lesbian condition has not yet found a sufficiently compelling literary voice (there are exceptions, of course, like Dorothy Allison's *Bastard Out of Carolina,* but they are generally books in which the lesbian theme barely surfaces), whereas it often appears as though everybody who is anybody grew up gay, male, and gifted and then went on to write a memoir or a novel describing how it was to grow up gay, male, and gifted.

Not long ago, in compliance with a request from a man I was trying hard to please, I went in search of a dildo. This man had pronounced that every woman's "wardrobe," as he put it, should contain one, although when I asked around among my friends, not one professed to owning this crucial article. So I arranged to go with a friend, who had researched an article on women pornographers and thus was a fount of knowledge on such things, to a women's sex shop called Eve's Garden. My friend described the store as "lesbianish" and joked uneasily that the two of us would be taken for gay by virtue of frequenting it. The store is located on Fifty-seventh Street in Manhattan, on the upper floor of an office building. When we got off the elevator and walked down a corridor to a door that could have been the door to anything—a dentist's office or a public relations firm—I remember thinking how like a woman it was to hide her erotic goods away from passersby, how unlike a man, who displays his sexual paraphernalia in the full light of day in a street-level boutique on Christopher Street.

Eve's Garden turned out to have a dingy, slightly sad atmosphere; it was a far cry from the bawdy, Rabelaisian emporium I had envisioned. There were sections of books and videos, with half of both these sections reserved for specifically lesbian themes, including a section on lesbian S&M. There were some cautious bondage-related devices for sale as well—a velvet eye mask, handcuffs, nipple clamps, and a leather-fringed paddle that looked as if it might be more useful for dusting than for inflicting pain. Most eye-catching, though, was the array of dildos and dildo-shaped vibrators in all colors and sizes, dildos so big they would make a man blush for his own endowment, cheap plastic ones and expensive latex ones.

I stood there and gaped, not knowing where to begin, other than with the conviction slowly forming in my mind that the problem of penetration—the wish to be filled by something hard and penislike and not female—would not go away, even for lesbians. Which realization brought in its wake another thought: Given that sex requires some antiphonal tension, and given, too, that sexual desire is partly a construction of the imagination, the suspension of disbelief that is required is far less when one of two men is asked to "play" a female—all he has to do is lie down and submit—than when one of two women must parody a man's role. Standing in Eve's Garden I picked up one dildo after another, smooth purple cones and flesh-toned striated ones—the more ambitious the level of emulation, the more expensive—and came back to the truth as it exists, inescapably, for me: I wanted the real thing.

The same friend who took me to Eve's Garden described a lesbian porn flick she had watched in which one woman performed oral sex on another woman's strapped-on dildo, said dildo having first been conscientiously fitted with a condom. This scenario suggests to me such a stupendous muddle of issues that I find it difficult to contemplate what it might hope to signify. Why, for instance, is safe sex—which I assume is being given its due with the condom—an issue between a woman and a rubber penis-substitute? What bothers me more is that I can't figure out who is supposed to be getting pleasure here, unless perhaps it's the dildo. And even if one were to grant that both women were getting pleasure out of their respective roles as fellatrix and fellated-upon, haven't we thereby worked our way back again to the tired conventions of heterosexuality and its Hegelian divisions of dominance and submission? And isn't the whole enterprise of lesbianism, or one of its salient departure points, meant to be a renegotiation of precisely such a reflexive division of power?

Just as the theater of a certain form of sadomasochistic encounter requires too many props for my erotic purposes, so does the proscenium of a certain form of lesbianism. But if the sight of two women playing at heterosexuality doesn't speak to me, the gentler kinder lesbianism—*sans* dildos and full of mutual loving caresses—speaks to me even less. Perhaps it comes down to no more than that I myself am not democratic enough in matters of the libido to be able to conceive of the possibility of an erotic charge occurring in a situation in which two people lie together and neither of them has a penis. I can conceive of great *emotional* intimacy occurring in such a situation, but sexual arousal for me hinges on an intimated imbalance of power, on someone having something that I want and don't already possess. The idea of being penetrated by a man excites me, if only because penetration promises a resolution of sorts, even if it is merely a resolution of my distrust of men.

Which comes first in the evolution of lesbianism—the fear of men? The desire for women? Or is it something else that seals a lesbian's sexual fate, something that has less to do with emotional tugs and amorous inclinations than with a vision of oneself snug in the harbor of female love?

· · ·

It seems to me that women, more than men, have always run the risk of having their sexual identity defined for them by others—*this* is how arousal happens, *this* is what an orgasm should feel like—if only because so much of what transpires with women goes on inside, away from direct observation. In Victorian times women were supposed to close their eyes and think of England, to suffer the ignominy of sex on behalf of their husbands and their country. In our own time, which is as intent on demystifying the notion of the taboo as earlier ages were on enshrining it, the touted delights of female masturbation have all but replaced the more interactive pleasures of copulation. (Perhaps because it has been acknowledged as a grungy compulsion all along, male masturbation has not been "discovered" as an erotic high point in quite the same way.) The proscriptive, in other words, has ceded to the prescriptive—and women are still being told what an orgasm should feel like and how best to achieve one! In the flurry of excitement about the brave new world of masturbation we may have lost sight of the fact that a transgressive act does not in and of itself provide sexual gratification; sometimes it provides nothing more than a taste of the formerly forbidden. Achieving orgasm through masturbation, once viewed as the province of men and then as the poor sister of orgasm à deux, may no longer be something to hide under the covers about, but it is not the same as being touched, licked, made love to by another human being.

There is no easy solution, so far as I can see, to what I call "the penetration problem." A woman has a hole where a man has a dangling something—this penis, this odd-looking, mercurial dildo-made-flesh, made susceptible to the waning and waxing of its possessor's desire—that can become erect and fill the hole up, thereby relieving her of her separateness, if only temporarily. This is also why two men together—but not two women—seem, quite frankly, to have all the sexual equipment they need between them, at least for the purpose of solving the penetration problem. The theory of penis envy in its literal Freudian form —which has always struck me as misbegotten, in any case, since most women regard the penis less as an organ to be coveted than as one to be borrowed as needed—may have been correctly scoffed into the shadows by feminist psychoanalytic thinking, but one is still left with the dictates, and the limitations, of human anatomy.

Finally there is this: I have always been fascinated by women. I collect them the way some women collect men. As a breed, I rate them more highly than I do men, and at dinner parties I tend to talk to the female seated on my left rather than to the male on my right. (I've often thought that one of the problems besetting the women's movement is that too many of its leaders seem to want to empower women without much liking them. At a book party I attended for Alice Walker some years ago, Gloria Steinem stood talking to my then-husband—he is, I admit, an attractive man—without so much as acknowledging my presence next to him.) I have never learned how to flirt properly with men, but with women I am a practiced seductress. I like to study my women friends, to learn their habits and their secrets. They, in turn, have offered me the sort of sustaining affection and nurturance without which life would be more of a misery than it is. By contrast, I have rarely been other than passingly friendly with a man I am not sexually involved with.

But if it is true to say I love women, it is equally true to say that I don't know how or, more correctly, don't wish to translate this affection into sexual terms. There is, I suppose, the option of bisexuality, but I remain convinced that this is an option which works well in real life rarely, if at all. In contrast to the concept of androgyny, which has always seemed liberating, demanding no more than that one accept the existence of the boyish in the girl or the girlish in the boy, real bisexuality—as opposed to a young woman's flirting with lesbianism on the way to heterosexuality, or an older woman's retreating to lesbianism after a failed marriage—

presupposes a flexibility and a greater tolerance of anxiety than most people have. I, at any rate, am surely not the one to give it a try. I'm sufficiently rattled when I wake up in a room not my own that the idea of waking up and not knowing on a given day whether the body beside me is male or female strikes me as a recipe for psychic disaster.

So there you have it, or at least you have what I've been able to make of my passion for women, this love that dares speak its name. Sometimes I find myself wondering whether all the interesting women I know are fooling themselves into loving men for the sheer personal challenge, and the social endorsement, of it, while each and every one of them is biding her time until she can figure out a better arrangement. Other times I wonder, had I been born into a more casually structured family or gone to college twenty years later, whether I would have tried to find out if a woman's tongue in my mouth tasted better first time around than a man's, or if a woman's fingers on my breasts could make my nipples stand up the way a man's fingers can. Meanwhile I make do with the painful strictures of being a woman who is not sure how much she likes men but who knows she needs them.

Is it a dare not taken, this bright red ball suspended in the air, forever uncaught? *Lesbian:* I still warm to the word, the slow-moving sound of it, that long first syllable—*lez*—ending on an enclosure, *bian.* What would it feel like to be a woman for whom it has never been a choice, never been anything but a conviction, sending her into the embrace of another woman, a woman with a body like hers, a synonym rather than an antonym? Have I chosen heterosexuality, with its impossible anxieties, or has it chosen me? Either way, it's the closet I'm stuck in.

Wives

by Heather Lewis

I got out of there, out of Beth's office. I went directly home and, once there, tried not to think of the only thing I could think of, which was when could I have her again.

It was a Friday, so I should've been going to work in the morning. I knew this much, though it didn't exactly mean I'd do anything about it.

When it came time, I called in sick, not realizing until afterward that I'd done the same thing the week before. Realized maybe I ought to begin worrying what they would think. I didn't earn enough there, and I hadn't been making money any other way lately. Something needed to change.

I lay in bed and tried to convince myself that Beth only meant trouble. That the thing to do was get away from her. Thinking this left me thinking about her, though. And once I'd begun to do that, the will to leave her didn't last long.

I told myself my concern was practical, that it was simply about legalities, that I needed to keep seeing her to meet the terms of my probation. This rationale was so thin that even I could see through it; they could have assigned me to another therapist. Still, I tried to stay on this plane and not drift into thinking about how she could make me feel, when she wanted to, which didn't seem often enough.

I couldn't face calling her. Spent the day—Saturday—avoiding this impulse. Finally went out to avoid it because I couldn't stand that she might play cool and aloof and impossible. That this weekend might completely match the last one, with me organizing my life around her, running to her and not knowing how I'd find her. I already had this sense that she took up too much of my life, or maybe all of it. And right when I needed badly for this not to be true, I ran into Burt.

This was not a hard thing to do. It was only a matter of going to certain places at certain times. And so I did these things believing I had no plan in mind.

He was at that same bar, with Jeremy this time. And I'd seen his car in the lot with the same guy waiting behind the wheel.

They asked me to sit at their table. Began buying me drinks, and all through this I kept wondering just what they wanted me for. They weren't talking to me really, not exactly. I was just there listening to them, and then they got up and we all went out and they gave me a ride home, which was good, since I still wasn't driving my car.

This put me pretty much where I'd been, only now it was later and I was drunk, and so my resolve was nowhere and I found myself calling Beth. She sounded sleepy and irritable but not quite surprised and so I couldn't help but feel she'd won.

I didn't ask to see her; not asking seemed like the only way to preserve some kind of dignity. This seemed to confuse her, and after all I hadn't called with anything else in mind, so we stumbled around awhile, and she finally said, "Why don't you meet me at noon?"

She said it in this in-between way that almost made me say where, and besides her office seemed too small and not right. We didn't say any more, and I went to sleep feeling, well, "happy" isn't quite the word, but secure maybe. Drunk, anyway.

I woke up later than I'd intended and with the sense of having made a mistake. I thought quite seriously of standing her up. Really wanted to, though the motive was flimsy, hard to determine, harder to act on.

I arrived at her office disheveled and discouraged. She was there already, and she came out to the waiting room and took my arm in a way that reminded me we hadn't always been like this, and we went into her room and sat down. I felt oddly comforted by this, unsure now what I wanted from her, and she seemed that way too, tentative and different.

I didn't say anything but found myself looking at her intently, meeting her eyes for what seemed like a long time. Then I noticed what I was doing and so my eyes found the floor and stayed there. And when she spoke, when she said, "Are you all right these days?" the sound of her voice made me jump. Any noise, really, would've startled me.

I didn't know how she meant this. How widely she meant it. How much ground I was allowed to cover if I answered. The easy thing would've been to say yes, I'm fine, but this was so far from true I couldn't shape the words. What I said instead was "I don't really think so."

I looked at her when I said it and wished I hadn't because it seemed to have hurt her. She maybe had wanted the other answer. How could I know what she wanted? And I was so weary of trying to know what was in her head and of her never letting on. This last thing, maybe, provoked me to say, "Are you?"

Her face changed again. She looked as if she had no idea what I'd said, and so I quickly added, "All right, I mean."

Her eyes went cloudy and then teared up, and my own vision blurred from the same things, and we just sat there staring at each other.

I wondered how to find the way through this, how to come out the other side and quickly. But just when I thought I'd be unable to stand this another moment, it grew sweet and I felt a closeness I hadn't felt in months. And while this feeling took over my body, while this sweetness roamed my chest and then the rest of me, taking hold in my limbs, I willed my brain to keep out of it, to stay still and not wreck it, not start me pumping to leave or push this toward sex, because of course those escapes were there too, always there and calling.

She didn't fidget, and she didn't look away. But she didn't say anything either. Not for the longest time. And then finally she said, "I'm afraid I'm not helping you."

I couldn't imagine how she meant this. I wanted to laugh, but she seemed genuine. Seemed not at all to see the absurdity of what she'd just said. This left me light-headed, nearly giddy, unsure that I could keep hold of what seemed maybe like anger.

There was so much room here for nastiness, for sarcasm. The only thing stopping me was the look on her face, still truthful and gentle. To meet that with cruelty seemed wrong. What I did instead was stall. I said, "How do you mean?" And I truly wanted to know, because the eeriest thing was the way I could never tell if she acknowledged all of what went on with us or if she kept it buried too deep.

"I think you're getting into trouble."

I wondered if she was talking about herself more than me—if she meant I was getting her into trouble—because now her eyes left mine and she stared out the window until this began to feel like all the other times she'd tried to keep herself away from me.

"How?" I asked her.

"You're going back to it."

"Not really, not that much. Not lately."

"Weren't you doing it just last night?"

This threw me. And when she looked back at me her eyes looked sore. I found myself trying very hard to see what she was saying in some other way than that she'd gone looking for me.

At first I thought she'd maybe seen my car in the parking lot, drawn her conclusions from there, but then I realized I hadn't driven it, and so what did that mean? That she'd actually been in that bar last night?

"I tried calling you," she said. "I wanted to see if you were okay. I hadn't heard from you. I was worried, and so I went by your place, but there were no lights and you didn't answer, but your car was there. I went to the train station because it was the only other place I knew to look."

She stopped here, as if this was too painstaking, too time-consuming. Her eyes drifted away, and when she started again she said, "I saw you with those men."

She said all of this as if it made sense, as if what she'd done was the most ordinary thing for a person to do. It was hard not to go along with her. Not to feel that, yes, of course, she's the one who knows what she's doing.

I kept my head just above water. I said, "What is it you think you saw?"

"I saw you get in a car with them."

I wanted her to look at me, wanted to get her to, because all I could see was her sitting in her car in that lot watching for me. I couldn't stand what this had me wondering, and it made me speak more directly than usual. I said, "Look at me," but when she did she seemed to be almost crying, so I looked away.

"So you thought up the rest of it, made it up," I said.

"Should I have stayed and watched?"

I wanted to ask her what she was doing there in the first place, because this all gave me too much to sort through. I felt unnerved and afraid of her and, at the same time, cared for—that she would go to such lengths, but out of what motive?

"They drove me home."

"Oh, and that's better?"

"No, that's it. That's all of it." I said this, not quite understanding how quickly I'd become the one defending my actions, though my response served both of us. It let her stay above question, and it let me not think what the questions should be.

I stole a look at her and then another, and when I was sure she'd gotten ahold of herself I kept looking. This put us back to staring at each other, which started hard and almost mean before it went gauzy. I wouldn't touch her. I kept telling myself this over and over in my head until I believed it, but I began to see my leaving as the only way to ensure it.

It wasn't me, but something about her that demanded I do this. I don't mean how it usually went, with her telling me to leave. This instead felt like "Get out before it's too late, this time might really hurt."

I did leave, and she didn't stop me. But I went home to find something I'd never have expected. Inside my building, just outside my door, Ingrid was sitting on the steps. The sight of her took away whatever will I'd ever had with her. And then, with Beth at my back, the sight of Ingrid felt like relief.

We went inside, and she stayed near the door, sort of hovering there as if she didn't know any better than I did why she'd come. I put my keys down. I took off my shoes without thinking, because my feet had begun to hurt from all the walking I'd been doing.

I sat on the couch and waited. Ingrid finally sat down, but she kept her coat on, looked confused with me or herself, I couldn't know which. Something looked even more wrong than usual, and this made me reach over and pull her coat off her shoulders, pull her toward me, and I held on to her while she cried, and I kissed her hair and just held her.

I didn't think I wanted to know what had happened—what on earth could've made her come here. I knew we'd wind up in the bedroom, but I hoped it'd take a while, because I was afraid of what I might find on her body.

It was bruises, all along her left side. The kind you get from someone getting you down on the floor and kicking you. She never said what had happened, never explained the bruises, but then, I suppose that's what I offered, someone she could go to without explanation. Someone who'd just simply know and know exactly.

We didn't really do anything more than lie around with each other. Finally I went to find some ice for her, though being only as far away as the kitchen gave me the distance to ask what jeopardy she'd put me in by coming here. And if she meant to begin making a habit of it? This appealed to me even as it frightened me.

I went back to her, laid a towel on her side and then the ice and then put some pillows around her, and all of this started me thinking about the way it'd been in their house. The way it had worked with her and me and her husband. Her cleaning up the mess he'd made of me, taking care of me afterward. And through the same kind of logic people seem to expect from me and even count on, I began to feel I owed her this. That she'd do the same for me. That she already had.

In the morning I had trouble with Ingrid even being there. I got up, took the towel away, now soggy and cold. I did these things trying not to wake her, and she went along with this, seemed dead to anything I might do, and I was glad for it.

I needed some time by myself. I needed at least to figure out what day it was and where I should be. It felt like Sunday, but knowing it wasn't did nothing to put me in motion.

It was late enough that the phone began ringing, and I knew it'd be my boss at the store trying to find me. That was about the last thing I could see dealing with, so I unplugged the phone. Decided right then I wouldn't go back to that job.

This meant spending the day with Ingrid. Maybe it did. After all, I didn't know her plans. How long she expected to stay. I'd remained in an in-between of not wanting her there and feeling closed in, but at the same time afraid of her leaving, not for her but for me. Afraid of being alone with myself in a way that might make me sort through the things I was doing.

Ingrid did stay. She spent the day in bed, not really ever awake. I waited on the couch, realizing finally that I missed my afternoon drinks, the ones that usually started at lunch. I pulled out a bottle and a glass and lay there drinking, watching Ingrid through the bedroom door.

About when I was getting dressed to go see Beth, Ingrid got up and went into the bathroom. And after she'd been in there for a while, I heard water running, heard what sounded like her getting into the tub, and I went in to brush my teeth.

"I have to go out for a bit," I told her.

And though she looked stricken, she pulled back from this, I guess, because her voice was steady when she said, "Would it be all right for me to stay here a few days?"

I considered this, knowing I would never refuse, but that alone wasn't enough to keep from figuring out where it would put me. Having her here while I went back to work for real in the parking lot? The way this would up the chances of her husband showing up looking for me? Or sending someone else to do it.

"You can stay as long as you need to . . . as long as you want to." This was what I finally told her. And when I began my walk to Beth's I saw my car as I passed the little lot by my building. I wondered if I should move it, put it somewhere else. Whether it could be something that would tip off Ingrid's husband all the faster to my whereabouts. But then, of course I knew he'd find us easily whenever he bothered to try.

I got to Beth's still edgy and distracted. I couldn't tell how she was, and it seemed like forever since I'd seen her, what with all that had happened in between. She looked different to me, but then, she did look different during the week. More distant and composed, even if just on the surface.

"You didn't go to work again."

She said this just as a statement of fact, while I was still standing, running my fingers over a glass paperweight full of trapped dead flowers. This object sat on her desk, and I was surprised to notice that I was standing right behind her— something I'd never done before. She didn't turn to look at me when she talked. Instead she looked straight ahead. Looked at the chair where I should have been sitting, and I might've sat down if I hadn't known that as soon as I did she'd find something else to look at besides me.

Having Ingrid in my home gave me some kind of false something. Bravado, I guess, because I felt that I needed Beth less, though I suppose I really needed her more, if only she'd been someone I could talk to.

I'd moved quickly to the other side of what I'd just been feeling. Began feeling so swiftly small and afraid that I did sit down, and when I did, I astonished myself. I said, "I think I'm in trouble."

She looked at me. For real she did. She said, "Tell me what's happened."

I had enough sense to know I couldn't do that, not exactly. I said, "I can't go back to that job. I just can't. There's too much else . . ."

I expected a lecture, something standard she'd shift into from habit, but instead she said, "Do you want to do the other thing more?"

"No, I don't think so. I don't know. I just know I can't play store any longer. I don't belong there. I don't know who I am there because I'm never there, not really, not me."

"Where do you belong?"

"I don't know. Maybe hooking suits me better. It's clearer."

I didn't know why I was saying these things to her, and I believed I'd better stop because it seemed dangerous. She might be dangerous if I let her know what really went on inside me.

I waited for her to argue with me, but she didn't. She said, "Why do you think that?"

"Because I know what to do, what's expected of me." And then I thought of Burt and said, "Most of the time, anyway."

I sat there unable to say anything more, and as I looked at her, this longing for her seeped into every space in me. It gave me a strange solid feel, but with a weight to it. I didn't believe I could get to my feet if I tried. But she was on hers and holding her hand out to me, and when we walked to her car, she kept her arm around my waist and I leaned into her and the heaviness of my body just felt pleasant.

She drove us to a park near her house. No one much was there, it being after dusk and cold out. I pulled the coat she'd given me tighter around me, and it was odd to be among swings and slides, things children played on, but the cold air felt good and she felt good, still with her arms around me, still guiding me around. The sweetness of all of this made me want to cry, and the funny thing of it was that's what I did.

I cried in her arms for what seemed like forever, until I really couldn't stand up anymore. And so we sat on a picnic table, her still with her arms wrapped around me. And then somehow it was time to get back in the car. I wanted her to turn down the street to her house, but she didn't. She drove me home.

My place did make more sense, what with her having a husband, but then here I was with someone else's wife, so what could I do? She said, "Will you be all right? Do you want me to come in with you?"

And of course I did. I wanted her more in that moment than maybe I ever had. And Ingrid? I couldn't tell Beth about her. There was nothing to do. I said, "No, I'll be okay. I'm all right." And then I said, "Thanks." And before I got out of the car I put my arms around her neck and held on for a little bit, and when I went upstairs I felt okay again. For a little while I really did.

. . .

Ingrid was dressed and seated on the couch. She really did look like a wife all of a sudden, and she'd somehow fixed us dinner or bought it somewhere, so we ate and had some drinks and it began to seem normal to have her there. And though I'm not proud of it, it crossed my mind she might take care of money for me for a while. Postpone my having to go out again.

We were still drinking and smoking when the phone rang. My instinct, of course, was not to answer it, but I knew it was Beth.

I picked it up and she said, "I just wanted to make sure you were all right."

I walked with the phone into the bedroom and closed the door to Ingrid, but I couldn't shift gears so fast. I heard the jerky guilt in my voice when I said, "I'm okay, really." And everything about the way I was speaking made plain my impatience. She couldn't know why, just sounded sort of confused, and she wound up saying, "Tomorrow, why don't you come later than we said?"

"When?"

"Six, I guess. That would be better, I think. I have a full day and . . ."

She didn't bother to finish. She just stopped, as if she remembered who she was talking to.

"Six is fine," I said. "I have some things to do, too." I didn't know why I'd said this last thing and wished I hadn't.

"Oh," she said. "All right. Six, then." And I felt her lingering, and it felt brutish to edge toward hanging up, but in another awful way it seemed to be working in my favor.

"Okay, I'll see you then," I said. And then I hung up the phone and went back to Ingrid.

She still sat on the couch, smoking a cigarette, staring at her drink on the coffee table.

"Who was that?" she asked, as if she'd had years of practice, which of course she had.

It startled us both, though. Her more than me because she

quickly said, "I'm sorry. I don't know why I said that. It's none of my business."

I didn't attempt to explain, though a part of me wanted to. Here I was again, with all of this inside me that I wanted to tell but with the absolute wrong person to tell it to.

Instead I held out my hand and she took it. We went into the bedroom, me not knowing who I wanted exactly, only knowing too clearly it was Beth who'd started me needing someone.

Ingrid and I lay down together, and it seemed at first as if it might be like last night, with us just lying around, and in a funny way recognizing that this was maybe what I wanted most from Beth—or would've tonight anyway—this drove me past it. I couldn't lie there thinking about her. If I did, I might start crying again, from that same place I didn't understand, and that would give Ingrid all the wrong sorts of ideas about me. I'd be the last thing she'd want.

I undressed her and then undressed myself, and she turned the covers down on the bed, which she must've made, and I wondered at what I was doing, not just this minute but with the whole of my life. Wondered how I'd come here and from where.

These thoughts must've stopped me entirely, because I heard Ingrid's voice. Heard her say, "Nina, what is it? What's the matter?"

And I discovered myself standing stock still by the bed, but breathing hard and wishing I'd told her my real name, because maybe then I'd feel as if we knew each other.

"Nothing," I said as I got under the covers with her. But it wasn't going to work; I knew that already. I couldn't get rid of all the things I was thinking, and when she began to touch me—at first just my neck, stroking a line under my jaw—I knew I'd never keep away from the feelings, either. And so, with neither my mind nor my body a safe place to be, I looked to her body. Turned toward her and began touching her in return, and for a short while this worked.

I kissed her shoulders and then her breasts. Did these things until all I felt was her and not me. And this lasted until I pulled the covers back, saw the bruises on her side, by now purply and still reddish.

The sight of them caught me up, nearly stopped me, and for an instant it ran through my mind to ask her how it'd happened. But I knew this too was about me. About keeping me from myself, and I knew it wouldn't work, and besides, I knew exactly how she'd come to be hurt in this way. I could see it all—her on the floor and him kicking her—and I knew that the one or two times I'd had that done to me I'd felt less human than ever.

To make her revisit this just to spare myself, it seemed close to something he might do. Instead, I put a pillow behind her so she wouldn't have to lie flat, and she sank against it while I wrapped my arm around her thigh.

I kissed her forever—her belly, her thighs—and I felt her hands in my hair, heard her saying little things, murmuring so that I couldn't make out her words and didn't quite want to, afraid it might sound too much like what Beth had said. And if they were both saying the same kinds of things, how could I believe either one of them? How could it be any more than the things people say when they're together like this? And this was made all the more tangled by my wanting to believe Beth but not Ingrid.

So in this way I came back to Beth just as I got inside Ingrid. And I listened to Ingrid now because it was only sounds and breaths, and my own breathing was changing but not in the right way. In a way, that forced me to take my mouth from her and just fuck her and try to choke off my own sounds, which might end up as sobs if I didn't get ahold of myself.

Ingrid tried to turn, first toward her bruises, but she cried out when that hurt, and so she turned toward me. I pulled another pillow, let her turn onto her stomach, got myself up and behind her, got my hand back inside her, with her asking all this time now for more of me, of my hand.

I grew afraid of myself in this, afraid I'd get carried away, carried off to where she wanted me to go, and then I stopped worrying about this.

I fucked her until she was the one who was crying—out of a place I knew and didn't know, because usually when she got here she stayed silent and away from me. But this time, when I started to pull away, she cried to me to keep on. She said, "Please, don't. Please don't leave me."

She'd never said anything like this, and so I listened. I put my hand farther into her and held it there, tried to get farther inside and she held herself very still, and then I did, too. I held her, still with my hand there, stayed just this way until she turned again, toward me, and her face looked a way I'd never seen. She looked young and afraid, and I opened my arms and she held on.

It was a long time before she quieted. I felt helpless. Thought of all the stupid things I could do—bring her a drink, a cigarette. I kept myself from doing these things until she got to the place of asking me to, and then I was glad to have actual tasks. To be able to get up from that bed.

I brought these things back with me—the bottle, our glasses. Made a separate trip for the cigarettes, just to have more time with myself. I tried to drink the way she did—in the long swallows that were helping her—but for me it just brought back the choking, and the cigarette I tried did this too, even more. I stubbed it out halfway finished, and that was when she noticed me.

She curled up near me and put her hand between my legs, and I lay back, opened my legs because she told me to, and it felt like what I wanted.

She stroked me and stroked me and I felt a calmness begin near her hand and then follow it. She trailed her fingers up my body to my throat and back down, and I couldn't not remember that Beth had done this too, and not so long ago. And so I wondered, What is it about me that lets women know to do this?

My breathing grew steadier and deeper, and she talked to me in a way that said nothing. She said things like "There, now. You're all right. Sweetheart, everything's all right." And I could see how it wasn't all right, because I'd begun to believe her, and when she put her hand in me I couldn't be anywhere else but with her. Couldn't do anything but feel what she was doing. And it was all slow and gentle, and I wanted more of her than I could take. Tried hard to ask for her, but now I was the one who could only make sounds and cries.

She knew anyway. We were enough alike in these ways, and so I felt her get very far into me and felt myself close around her, wanted to put my legs around her too but couldn't move them. I felt limp and wonderfully exhausted, so slack and peaceful, and she seemed to find comfort in this, because when I looked, she was smiling. Not in a large way, but this small change in her face that I hadn't seen in a long while, or maybe ever.

She took her hand from me slowly, let it stay underneath her when she sank into me. And I felt her hand and the weight of her body as indistinguishable things. And I came in this way too, a way that made it hard to make out what was what and who was who. But all that really mattered right then was that somebody was holding me.

An excerpt from *Trilogy*

by Sapphire

Go head, pretty baby, honey knock yourself out. . . .
                                          —Jimmy Reed

P is for Princess, the Original Bronze Beauty of Show
World. It's for pretty titties, generosity, and a weird honesty. I
remember the first time I saw her, she had on a long Indian-
looking wig, cheap sharp vines, makeup, heels swishing, hostile, arrogant. Sixteen. Holding her windows. A peep show
queen. Uh-huh, a freak for white boys, blonds. Hated niggers.
Shocked me with her sickness. Told me she hated black men,
niggers. I was still new, able to be shocked, not in total understanding, not knowing the circle unbroken I would end up
well worked and insane too. And we became close. She was
real. I liked her body. It was me, Sherry, Naomi, Lee,
Princess, Misty, Angel, Zulima, Shawneesy, RubyJune—
stripping, jammed into that little dressing room, a world to
itself, a freak set untouched by outside values. I learned to be
free, to like their bodies, play. The men in the booths, the
freaks, I watched them drop quarters, crook their fingers,

beckon, unzip their pants. Sticking out their tongues, pointing to their dicks, *Oohh,* they would go as they begged us to
look, as if it was something good. We laughed at them as they
looked at us. They jacked off, rolling their eyes, shaking,
pissing in the booths. Rasta men, Hasidic Jews, Asian busi-
nessmen, slick young-looking niggers, bowing before a need
in the booth. We needed the money.

I was new in town. The dude I was staying with, who was
a friend of my girlfriend's new boyfriend, worked there as a
projectionist, first took me there. I was wigged, made up, told
Lee, the manager, yes, I had danced, could dance, would au-
dition. She told me okay, but she didn't need no dancers, not
till October, but I needed then. She told me she needed a
"love team" now. I said, Cool. I had a partner, I told her. The
dude I was staying with told me about a dude he knew was
game. We hooked up. Money. I needed money. We "re-
hearsed" at his ol' lady's house. Came back. Lee said we was
a good love team. She liked us. She used me in between my
love-team act too. I would go out there and dance with the
girls, help 'em do their shows. It was fun, but she didn't pay
me. Lee ran so much game trying to get sales up. Worked us.
She was a big Hottentot butt woman, ex-secretary/singer
who'd slipped into the business. She told everyone she was a
virgin. I don't know, it sounded weird to me. I never said anything, she was responsible for the paychecks, the bookings. I
held on to my dreams, talked, found myself to be like everybody else. Whatever else I thought, I was still there showing
pussy like everybody else.

It was another world. Naomi—nineteen, she said—was
Puerto Rican but swore on nine Bibles she was Polynesian.
Told me she was from Polynesia. But I know the South
Bronx when I see it. That girl was obsessed with the buck.
Said she wanted to get twenty grand in the bank. She worked
her ass off from ten in the morning to twelve at night, some-
times three in the morning. Only took off to get costumes,
makeup, go to the bank or to Mass. The bitch went to Mass

on Sunday, and Lee, too, religious like that, but you know, Naomi swore she wasn't gay. Too hard, she protested, too hard. I knew better. Her and Sherry became lovers. It was a fantasy world, the women. Actually we only made three dollars and fifty cents a show and usually only did one show an hour—that we got paid for, that is. Lee had us out there humping a lot for free, "doubling" she called it. "Why don't you help so and so? She's losing her windows." But we worked twelve hours a day, seventeen on weekends, and lots of times there were too few girls so we'd get in a lot of extra shows. It wasn't nothin' to come out with four, five bills a week, but still . . .

Misty and I, we liked each other. We all did teams together—lesbian love teams. It was fun. I liked doing it with Sherry, Princess, Misty. Not Naomi so much, though. She twisted, flipped like a fish. She always perfumed her pussy. I didn't like that. We usta freak off on the mike while we was doin' teams. Talk crazy shit like fuckin' Dobermans and a little house in the country, just my woman and me. And ooh, fist-fuck me, beat me. Crazy stupid shit. Sometimes the customers liked it, sometimes they didn't. One time me and Sherry was onstage and I was saying something like, "Do it to me wit a bottle, honey." I mean regular routine bull. And Misty rushed out onstage like a mad thing with a Coke bottle. Weird. Maybe she was high. "So you want a bottle?" She was serious. I had to use all my strength, she woulda jammed me if she could. I felt different toward her after that. Me and Sherry both said later, Whew! She's a little off. She was really serious!

Golden showers! The customers wanted to see golden showers. I pissed on Princess once on stage. I felt weird after that. She said, "Lemme do it to you." I said no. I know how she felt. Tina, this white broad, one of the manager's girlfriends, asked me to pee on her too. She was for real, heavy into S&M, usta come to work with bruises. That's how she got off. She was around forty, yeah, at least. She had kids, three or four of them.

Pornography is a trip. No big thing. We all got freak in us. Men are so weird. The dudes who come in those booths— slaves like. I'm glad my sex thang ain't like that. I'm glad I ain't got to pay.

Christina Dawn Santana was thirty-eight. She'd come out and tell you how old she was. She was a trip. Boy, that bitch could suck a dick. I had never seen a woman like that before. She blew my mind. She had a crush on the dude I was doing the love team with, would ask me to let her do my shows. I'd be glad. I hated it. She loved it. Didn't like to fuck, though. She was only into oral sex. She'd suck him off, then parade around the stage flexing her biceps. She'd make him come again and again. We watched amazed. I had never seen such a voracious woman. He begged off. He was drained, dry, weak. She exhausted him. I had never seen that before, always I had seen niggers begging for more. Christina would get drunk offa that rum. She liked me. But I couldn't relate. Uh-uh, not my thing. Now Zulima, she was fine. Built, brown-skinned, solid, lesbian to her heart. Dressed nice. A data processor during the day, love teams at night. Couldn't stand it, either, talked about how it feels to be a lesbian and have a man's hands on you four, five, ten, twelve times a day! I ate her pussy onstage, no fake simulation shit, we got on down! She turned out to be into masculine types, though.

The real bosses was Mafia men, least that's what everybody said. We didn't see 'em, though. A lot of the employees, projectionists, and shit was foreigners, West Indians and Africans, too. Show World didn't take taxes outta the girls' checks and we, most of the girls, used phony names and Social Security numbers. Misty was married to an East Indian dude darker than me who hated niggers. Both of Angel's parents were Black Muslims. She was born a Muslim, married a white Irish dude. Shawneesy married this French-Canadian dude named Peter. It used to trip me out—the black girls and white men. Now I understand. I understand good. Wigs, costumes, toenails, and G-strings. Music. Isaac Hayes sing some sexy songs. We usta play the hell outta Isaac Hayes. You could drown in the business. It's like dope or jail. Some people get in and never get out. Either way you're never the same.

4

On Passing and Solidarity

Queer in the Streets, Straight in the Sheets : Notes on Passing

by Ann Powers

T he afternoon I made my discovery I was sitting under a blazing spring sun in an Asian-food mall frequented by grad students and other Berkeley coeds, discussing gender trouble with two women friends. In the nineties, talking theory almost always means talking sex, and our conversation drifted from the fine points of phallocentricity to the merits of electric dildos over the battery-operated kind. We sparred, sharing insights but also competing over realness. Selene, who sleeps with women, expressed disgust at older feminist faculty members' delicate views of lesbian sexuality. Diana concurred, but felt the need to qualify, since she sleeps with men. So she concocted an astounding bit of logic. Citing an admired friend, a hot-shot activist and theory head, Diana said, "She told me I'm the queerest person she knows."

I'd just witnessed the emergence of the queer straight, that testy love child of identity politics and shifting sexual norms. The political impact of a rejuvenated gay and lesbian movement, coinciding with the latest of America's occasional crushes on all things androgynous, and even some things homosexual, has lit a match to the hierarchy of sexual preference. While hardly toppling the power structure, these shifts have inspired a certain deference to queers in leftist and bohemian circles. More quietly, they've sparked a series of defections from the straight fold. But not necessarily into gay sex. This queer way of being takes shape outside the bedroom.

At first, it may have seemed like a splash made by Madonna and Sandra's double dip—but the queer straight thing has begun to permeate the culture. After Nirvana's same-sex smooch fest on *Saturday Night Live,* Kurt Cobain declared himself "gay in spirit" if not in practice. More recently, Brett Anderson of Suede identified himself as a bisexual who hadn't yet had an experience with a man. The rise of mass drag, from *SNL* to U2, muddies the boundary between gay culture and straight appropriation. And the movie we're all sick of discussing, *The Crying Game,* can be seen as a psychological study of the queer straight under the gun.

After my brief run-in with Diana's queer straight sensibility, I began to notice similar attitudes up and down the Coast. Nattily attired academic climbers led panel discussions on homosociality in the beatnik scene and the films of John Wayne, affecting camp attitudes as they stole kisses from their girlfriends in the hall. The organizers of an annual northern California feminist conference drank at girl bars after planning sessions, flirting madly until they headed home to their male couch-potato mates. Straight marchers at domestic-partner rallies dared to chant, "We're here! We're queer! Get used to it!" Women sick of being harassed by guys, even cute ones, congregated in gay clubs, grooving with each other on the dance floor.

These queer straights would probably be horrified to think their behavior might translate as a tease. They mean to practice what theorists call "gender performativity," the act of defining your sexuality through manner and style. Postmodernism's logic of surfaces has turned the closet inside out, making the projection of a queer attitude enough to claim a place in homosexual culture. Yet queer straights don't practice the fundamental acts of intimacy that ground homosexual identity. They are neither bisexual nor experimenting. They're not ambiguously defined companions of gay men, as were the fag hags of yore. Queer straights don't just hang around; what they do is pass. They carefully maneuver their rhetoric toward ambiguities of desire and display, leaving aside questions of the private. "We're the perfect couple," a friend with queer straight tendencies gushed. "Everyone thinks I'm a lesbian, and everyone thinks Jake's gay."

As any eager student can attest, theory often leads to practice. Circumstances in my own life have pushed me toward this shaky ground. At Berkeley I read Judith Butler's dissections of gender as performance and Eve Kosofsy Sedgwick's ruminations on the homosexual continuum. (Sedgwick herself was a pioneer of this lifestyle, declaring herself "a sexual pervert" and therefore queer, although she is married to a man.) It wasn't long before my forays into politics and nightlife led me to queer circles. With activist girl pals, I started spending sweaty nights at San Francisco clubs like Uranus and Faster Pussycat; for stimulating sexual images that came anywhere close to resembling my own body, I turned to the lesbian porn magazine *On Our Backs*. Although not as adventurous as some friends who explored the North Mission jack-and-jill-off scenes—masturbation sessions involving people of all persuasions—I discovered the polymorphous possibilities of L.S.'s traveling Club Fuck!, where any flirtation could lead to a caress without further consequence. Yet I maintained a primary relationship with a man.

Just before I moved to New York, I attended a screening of Sadie Benning's videos at the San Francisco lesbian and gay film festival. I thought to myself, These dykes have the only style going in this town. A few days later I had my hair cut above my ears in a style not far from Benning's own. By the time I made it east, without my boyfriend, beginning a new career phase as an outspoken feminist critic, I was passing for queer virtually all the time.

"Why would you ever want to pass?" my dear friend Martin muttered incredulously into the phone after my announcement that I was writing this piece to comprehend my slip into "queerness." His disdain was understandable; he'd recently been outed in his very conservative workplace, and was undergoing scrutiny. Generally open about his identity, Martin nonetheless suffered the pain of stigma during his adolescence; the inability to fit himself into the comfy lifestyles of many heterosexual friends; the knowledge that his desire to have a child might never be satisfied, even through adoption; and a tragic distance from his family, from whom he hides his lovers and his lifestyle. These are still the costs of being gay in America, and there are others that damage even more severely—to the point of murder.

Queers often show suspicion and anger at straights who infiltrate their space. In the face of hatred from many heterosexuals and a history of marginalization on the Left, this hostility is completely justified. Furthermore, assimilation by straights can diffuse the focus of queer culture and politics, not to mention plain old hedonism. "You know what happens to a gay club when straights start coming," said Martin. "It becomes a straight club."

In addition, the notion of passing has connotations for queers—and for people of color—that hardly suggest liberation. At best, escaping from an oppressed identity by assuming a more acceptable one demands denial; at worst, it leads to self-hatred. Then there's passing racially in the opposite direction. Posing as a "white Negro" became fashionable in the 1950s, when bohemians thought they'd conquered racism by identifying African-Americans as more virile and expressive in their noble savagery. The current wave of lesbian and gay chic mirrors this reverse racism, as it ascribes tempting attributes such as hot sexuality, tragic courage, and devastating wit to homosexuals—traits that have historically been linked to inferiority and exclusion. Forbidden fruit attracts the Puritan; it always has.

Yet some straights passing for queer aren't just commandeering fabulousness or looking for a momentary respite from their own conflicted desires. They're hoping to lose their straight identity and maybe even find themselves. My own experience started with the not-so-noble wish to be accepted in situations that attracted me because they felt not only less repressive but far more vital than those dinner parties and double dates so common in straight circles.

Soon enough, however, I discovered that queer responses to sexual and domestic conventionality completed the choices I was making, despite my continued attraction to men. Imagining myself as a Queer Straight, I discovered the serious differences I have with the trajectory upon which I'd thoughtlessly been traveling. In these moments, passing became a passage into a whole new conception of the self.

I also realized that queer politics spoke to me and my peers more eloquently than any other grassroots movement. In the 1980s, ACT UP and Queer Nation revitalized street protest, mixing righteous rage with postmodern style and media savvy. Most important for twenty-whatevers who viewed the Left as a fortress of 1960s hippie values doled out by patronizing elders, queer groups offered politics that felt completely of the moment. When the Women's Action Coalition shot feminism some new sparks last year, the model it offered came directly from ACT UP. Although many of WAC's women are straight, the group's street actions and participation in events such as this year's march on Washington show a willingness to follow the example of queer display.

Learning the gay movement's methods has enriched feminism. And supporting queer causes is imperative for anyone who believes in personal freedom, especially with an enemy as formidable as the religious right. But identity politics has its problems: while it gives power to previously excluded voices, it also weakens our ability to connect with others who are different from us. Passing for queer is a nervous attempt to challenge these boundaries while honoring them. It's an undercover job that aims to subvert both the sickness of homophobia and the overwrought response of separatism.

The urge to pass comes from wanting to touch upon another's reality in ways that no amount of thinking or discussion can reach. I experienced this craving for unity out in the Riot Grrrl contingent at the Queer March on Washington. I felt that blood-sister tie. In a black bra and sunscreen, strolling with a companion who's just as uncomfortable as I am trying to squeeze into the corset of straight well-being, I had a revelation of what this march was for: sexual and personal freedom that transcends any category. The truckful of undergrads we'd carted to Washington made eyes at every baby dyke in sight. One girl wandered blissfully among the crowds, calm and confident, smiling at the vibe. Much later, as we were about to head home, she mentioned her boyfriend as if he were an afterthought. He lives in another city, she said; sometimes it's really tough. In her murmured sentences, I could hear my own divided self. We were sisters, all right, making a fragile attempt at some new truth.

"I respect queer space," one friend said the other day, when I asked how she handled her own double life. She has slept with women, but is currently in a long-term relationship with a man. For her, respect means no public displays of affection with the boyfriend. But, she might have added, no tricky attempts to claim similar experiences of oppression in the name of alternative lifestyles that really still conform to heterosexual norms, and no demands that straights be acknowledged as an equally important group within queer politics. Just as whites in the African-American civil rights movement needed to recognize the racism that ran through them as an inheritance, so must straights accept that the modes of sex and romance in which they still participate carry the seed of homophobia. The well-meaning slogan "Straight But Not Narrow" misses the point: a full embrace of queer culture wouldn't expand the boundaries of straightness; it would dissolve them.

The delicate line between homophobic, homo-huggy, and homo-emergent has long been a nerve center within the feminist movement. "We can't be truly honest and real with a straight woman," wrote the Gutter Dyke Collective in its 1973 manifesto. Another 1970s separatist group, Alice, Gordon, Debbie & Mary, wrote of being betrayed by women experimenting with lesbianism who later retreated into heterosexual bonds: "It is not up to lesbians to show straight women how not to oppress us. In fact, the simplest way for straight women to not oppress us is to give up their heterosexual privilege and join us."

The assertion that straight women may prove too ambivalent to trust has been expressed as recently as 1991 when, in the pages of *Ms.,* Kay Leigh Hagan compared straights to "orchids in the Arctic." While she allowed that they could also be feminists, Hagan noted that "it is important for heterosexual women to respect the fact that, metaphorically speaking, lesbians definitely log more time in the tropics." Suspicion also shadows the Lesbian Avengers' statement, in their manifesto published this year [1994], that they "believe in recruitment. Not by the army; not of straight women."

The mainstream women's movement deserves every ounce of the anger that lesbians feel at having been erased from view. But the view of women's nature propagated by separatists and cultural feminists is notoriously idealized, misrepresenting lesbians as well as straight women. At least one useful idea, however, has arisen from this conception: that of a lesbian continuum, as defined by Adrienne Rich. Working from historian Carroll Smith-Rosenberg's discovery of a nineteenth-century "female world of love and ritual" in which married women maintained lifelong romantic friendships with each other, Rich counted the many ways in which women eroticize their bonds. Through a litany of examples ranging from adolescent girl-crushes to older women's domestic companionship, we can see, in Rich's words, "breaths of female history and psychology that have lain out of reach as a consequence of limited, mostly clinical, definitions of 'lesbianism.'"

This description of a lesbian continuum immediately received flak from women who viewed it as an attempt to "free" lesbianism from the onus of sex. In California, pro-sex feminists such as Susie Bright, Pat Califia, and Dorothy Allison began producing often graphic expressions of politically incorrect desires, proving that no fuzzy dream of a woman's world can tame the realities of lust. Instead of cooling down what was simmering among women, pro-sex feminism heated everything up, emphasizing that fun could be had in any variety of ways, from cruising the sex-toy emporium Good Vibrations with a female buddy to renting Fanny Fatale's amazing ejaculation video to stripping down to your bra on Faster Pussycat's dance floor. The lesbian continuum overflowed into all corners of this feel-good atmosphere, as women discovered girl-love wherever they could find it.

Undoubtedly there were controversies among women in this community to which I, a straight whose passing went only so far, was not privileged. But that scene helped me understand ways in which my starstruck, sensual friendships with women during my teens and early twenties counted as love, even though we never made it into the sack. Passing, I realized that sex didn't have to mean going all the way, that in fact sex was being redefined all around me as the expansive and ever-present field of physical and spiritual growth it really always had been.

That's the way high theory, such as Judith Butler's notion of gender parody, works on the ground. As Butler notes, the point of drag—and, I would argue, of the queer straight experience—is to contradict the reality of an original, or natural, way of being female or male, homo- or heterosexual. As AIDS has pushed sex of all kinds out of the bedroom and into the realms of exhibitionism and fantasy, each of us can demonstrate a new fluidity in the way we touch each other, and uncover seemingly contradictory, but actually newly possible, aspects of ourselves.

When I moved across the country to live alone, my four-year romance transformed into a long-distance phone bill with no permanent reunion in sight, I discovered ways in which I didn't fit the straight norm that I'd inherited. I'm twenty-nine, unmarried, childless, and intending to stay that way. My primary political loyalties are to other women. In the past, I have been promiscuous and celibate, both by choice. I've been called a "fucking dyke" by men on numerous occasions, for refusing their advances, protecting my women friends, or simply standing up for myself. I never want to live in the suburbs, and at least half the time, I'd rather go dancing with my gal pals than cuddle up on the couch with a video, a pint of Ben & Jerry's, and my favorite guy.

It's not my right to claim a wholly queer identity. I've never verbally identified myself as a lesbian, and when push comes to shove in a conversation, I'll immediately confess my sexual preference for men. But I've learned much in my moments of passing, which have shifted from accidental to deliberate and back again. Where I've landed is somewhere in between, a no-woman's-land ready for discovering.

Conceptual Lesbianism

by Dorothy Allison

"I'm not yet a lesbian," the letter began.

Not yet? I passed the page over to my friend Jan. "What the hell do you think this is supposed to mean? You think maybe it's something she hasn't gotten around to, like putting henna in her hair or trimming her toenails? Or maybe she thinks of lesbianism as a trip she's always planned to take—like a day trip out to Coney Island or a really complicated expedition to the Himalayas or maybe to Montana?"

Jan gave me one of those looks that clearly expressed she knew I knew what the woman meant, all the different things she had implied. The letter, after all, had been written to accompany a review copy of the woman's book of poetry. And Jan was right. I could easily imagine the woman sitting down with a stack of magazines and newspapers or a list out of one of the directories of writers and reviewers, wondering how she was going to get anybody interested in excerpting or reviewing her work. Maybe she had come to my name after hours of work and had been feeling both tired and silly.

There had probably been different letters for different categories of reviewers, but I doubted she had sent one off to the *Guardian* that said "I'm not yet a socialist." Nor could I imagine such a letter from a male writer wherein he would define himself as "not yet a faggot." Even the radical fairies and men's movement theorists don't talk about conceptual homosexuality as the goal of a heightened sensitivity. But lesbians have had to confront a world of misconceptions, from our teenage years when they told us it was just a phase, to the last few years when magazines have prominently featured pretty young white female pairs and suggested that we're all some variation on k.d. lang, Martina Navratilova, or Melissa Etheridge—somehow establishing a notion in the public mind that lesbians are young, healthy middle-class jocks who can sing.

Ever since I heard the Ti-Grace Atkinson quote about feminism being the theory and lesbianism the practice, I've been uncomfortable with the odd glamour applied to the term "lesbian." I use the word "glamour" deliberately, since I believe that what has grown up around the concept of lesbianism is not only an illusion of excitement, romance, and power, but an obscuring mystery. Or, as a nasty lady I used to adore would always joke, "When is a lesbian not a lesbian? When she's a feminist!"

In the early days of the women's movement, many women found themselves struck dumb by the accusation of lesbianism: "Ah, you're all a bunch of dykes!" Some of these women made a practical and moral decision to confront the basis of the prejudice. After the first roll of "Oh, no, we're not," they started saying, "So what if we are?" Or at least some of them did. While parts of the women's movement did everything they could to disassociate themselves from anything remotely queer, just as they continue to do today, other feminists made a conscious and political decision to identify publicly with lesbians. In doing so they brought to question, in a way they had never intended, what it meant to be queer in this society. I am thinking not so much of the attention given to women like Kate Millett, who came out to wild press coverage and attack, but of women like Ti-Grace Atkinson and Robin Morgan. The former framed sex in so-cial-political terms, and the latter insisted on her right to call herself a lesbian, and not a bisexual, while committed to her marriage, husband, and son.

I was in Tallahassee, Florida, in 1974, a photographer's as-sistant and community activist trying to be a female version of the happy homosexual I had read about. The conceptual war being fought on the issue of lesbianism had a major im-pact on my life, though at first all I wanted to know was who was really a lesbian and who was not. But I read Ti-Grace Atkinson, Shulamith Firestone, the Furies Collective, and countless raggedy newsletters from Radical Feminists and began to rethink who I was and what I could do as a lesbian activist. Eventually my women's group and I decided that Charlotte Bunch's statement, "No woman is free unless she is also free to be a lesbian," was the perfect way to frame women's struggle for autonomy. It did not matter then who was really queer. It only mattered that we all challenge the boundaries of what was acceptable behavior and what was perverse.

Right.

Unfortunately there seemed to be a discrepancy between my personal life and my politics. I discovered, painfully, that this blurring of the definition of lesbianism led to a few prob-lems: regardless of how hard we tried to pretend that there was no difference between women who slept with men and women who slept with women, there did seem to be differ-ences. For one thing, I noticed that although there were lots of lesbians working to get the child-care center established at Florida State University, there were no heterosexuals working to get the same university to recognize the lesbian peer counseling group. Nor were we supposed to identify ourselves as lesbians when we applied for funding for the women's center itself. Very quickly, in fact, "feminist" seemed to become a code word for "lesbian," at least as far as the heterosexual population of Tallahassee was concerned. At the same time, saying you were a feminist at the local gay bar made many of the older lesbians nervous. "Yeah, but are you a lesbian?" I was asked, and began to suspect that something more than semantics was being confused.

Then I fell in love. Well, it might have been lust. I never got it all sorted out because the passion of the moment ran aground pretty quickly. Joanna was older than I was, served on the board of the women's center and the local land co-op, raised honeybees and goats, and drove a VW van with a sleeping bag perpetually unrolled in the back. She had long hair but wore it tied back all the time and was never seen in anything but blue jeans, high-top canvas sneakers, and T-shirts. I found her tremendously sexy and tried to tell her so one night after we'd finished putting tile down on the floor of the newly funded day-care center.

"Hnnnn." Joanna's mouth gaped open, and her face flushed a dark rose color. She looked away from me and started picking at the frayed cotton threads on the knees of her jeans. I told myself she was shy and sat quietly waiting for her to get over it.

"I do like you," she said finally, but her voice was uncertain and strained. We both waited. There's no telling how long we might have sat there if my friend Flo hadn't walked in. Joanna jumped up and announced that she had to go feed her goats. Flo looked at me curiously.

"What's wrong with her?" she asked, once Joanna was gone.

I didn't know. For a few weeks I suffered all the miseries of an early Ann Bannon heroine, mooning over Joanna while she avoided me. She must be in love with someone else, I told myself, and she was: a myopic, shaggy-haired guy out at the land co-op who had the plot of land next to Joanna's.

"I'd marry him, except he don't believe in marriage," Joanna told me finally, months after I had stopped tensing up every time she entered the room. "And I do like you," she said again. For the first time I understood the awkward emphasis on "do." We were eating pizza and sipping beer at one of the local student hangouts, surrounded by noisy fraternity boys and the celebrating members of the women's volleyball league. Joanna rubbed at her eyebrows with both hands and peered at me nervously. "Thing is, I just couldn't get myself around to doing anything with you. I mean, I can't even think about it without giggling." She promptly giggled. "I mean, I know I should be able to love you as easily as Charlie, make love to you, I mean." I watched that familiar blush creep up from her neck to her eyebrows. "But it just an't happening. You know?"

I nodded. I was feeling almost as embarrassed as she was. I had never slept with a straight woman in my life, and the thought made my stomach flutter. All I could say to Joanna was that the whole thing had been a misunderstanding. I didn't want to tell her that she looked like a dyke; I didn't know how she'd take that, and I didn't want any of my friends to think I had been pursuing her. Maybe if we had done something about it, the idea wouldn't have seemed so disconcerting to me, but the notion that my tentative flirting had made Joanna's stomach feel the way mine did at that moment—that was simply awful. I watched Joanna take another sip of beer and lean forward.

"But you know something?" she said. "It certainly got Charlie going. He's been just major enthusiastic since I told him."

I felt my own cheeks flame. "You told him about me?"

"No, no." Joanna looked indignant. "I didn't say who. I just kind of told him there was a woman interested in me. He an't got no business knowing who." I felt a little better at that, but she didn't stop. "But he did like the idea. Only I think he

likes it more that I didn't do it than if I had. You know?"
   Right.

At Sagaris, the feminist institute held in Vermont in 1975, I
ran into a number of women who labeled themselves "political lesbians." They didn't actually have sex with women, at
least not with any great enthusiasm. None of them seemed to
think that sex was a priority. They loved women and felt that
men were pretty hopeless—at least until after the revolution.
In fact, one of them told me, maybe all sex was just too prob-
lematic right now. She was pretty much celibate, although
she felt that she should still call herself a lesbian. Didn't I
agree?
   I didn't. I was starting to have serious doubts about this
whole concept. All right, in 1975 it was painfully obvious that
there were tactical advantages to having all these woman-
identified women running around. It seemed to ease the passage of some women through the coming-out process, as
well as providing a measure of safety for those lesbians who
could not afford to be publicly out. It also gave a major theoretical boost to making lesbian rights an issue for organiza-
tions like NOW. I liked the theory of the woman-identified
woman, liked watching women make other women the priority in organizing for civil rights, liked that even heterosexual women were beginning to see, on a day-to-day level, that
treating other women badly was no longer socially acceptable. I knew that the issues were connected, but it still made
me uncomfortable. All that talk about the woman-identified
woman was taking the sexual edge off lesbianism, and I was
sure I didn't like that.
   Political lesbians made the concepts of lust, sexual need,
and passionate desire more and more detached from the definition of lesbian. The notion that lesbians might actually be
invested in having orgasms with other lesbians, that lesbians
might like to fuck and suck and screw around as much as gay
men or heterosexuals did, became anathema.

By the late seventies, I was tracking the progress of the spiritual lesbian, a close cousin of the political lesbian, perfectly woman-identified and adamant about what was and was not acceptable practice for the rest of us. She wasn't goal-oriented (didn't really care if she came, just liked to cuddle), didn't objectify other women (never squeezed her lover's ass and breathed, "God, I'd love to get my hands in your pants"), and didn't lie awake nights mourning her inability to find true love or her constant obsession with sex and the lack of it in her life. The spiritual lesbian was a theoretical creature and a lesson to us all, not about what we were but about what we must not be.

This stuff gets confusing. I remember going to political gatherings—right now I'm thinking of the matriarchy conference in New York City in 1979—where lesbians, because of their detachment from males and male-identified precepts, were accorded a kind of rarefied status that seemed roughly equivalent to a state of grace. But much like the state of grace I was taught about in Baptist Sunday school, the one ascribed to lesbians was pretty ephemeral and unsubstantial. It evaporated as soon as one displayed any actual sexual desire, since lust seemed to be evidence of male-identification. At that same conference, I watched one of the speakers become extremely indignant at a lesbian who raised questions from the floor, a young woman whose main affront appeared to be the fact that she was wearing a button-down shirt and a tie.

"I think we're in trouble," I told a friend standing with me after the woman with the tie walked out followed by half a dozen women easily recognizable to me as not-at-all theoretical lesbians.

My friend just smiled. "When are we not?" she joked, and she was right.

The theoretical lesbian was everywhere all through the eighties, and a lot of times I could have sworn she was straight. Speaking on college campuses, identifying myself as a feminist and a lesbian but not an antipornography activist, I kept running into young women who knew who the lesbian was. The lesbian was the advanced feminist, that rare and special being endowed with social insight and political grace. I argued that there was a gap between their theory and my reality—that there were lots of lesbians who fucked around, read pornography, voted Republican (a few anyway), and didn't give a damn about the National Organization for Women. The lesbian you're talking about, I would try to explain, is the rage of all women, perhaps, but the lust of few. Real lesbians are not theoretical constructs. We have our own history, our own issues and agendas, and complicated sex lives, completely separate from heterosexuality, and just as embattled and difficult for straight society to accept as they ever were.

I do not believe that identity is conceptual. I am a lesbian and a feminist. I am not a paragon of political virtue, not endowed with an innate sense of feminist principles. My political convictions are hard-won and completely rooted in my everyday life. I can't sing. My hand-eye coordination is terrible; I'm legally blind for driving purposes. I am way past young, not very healthy, born working-poor, and fighting hard to acquire a middle-class patina, but I seem unable to change any of my working-class attitudes and convictions. I have never been monogamous, except in a de facto fashion these last few years when I just haven't had the time and energy for any serious flirting. Contrary to rumor and assumption, I don't hate men. I have never found them sexually interesting, though. I cannot imagine falling in love with a man. Nor do I believe that sexual orientation is something one can construct, that people can just decide to be lesbians or decide not to be—for political, religious, or philosophical reasons, no matter how powerful. I don't know if sexual preference and identity is genetic or socially constructed. I suspect it's partly both, but I do believe that there are people who are queer and people who are not, and that forcing them to change their innate orientation is a crime, whether that orientation is homosexuality, lesbianism, bisexuality, or heterosexuality. I believe that sexual desire is a powerful emotion and a healthy one. I'm pretty sure that when people acknowledge and act on their desire, it does us all some good—even if only by giving other people permission to act on their desire—that it is sexual repression that warps desire and hurts people.

All of these statements sound very simple, almost trivial, but it is a simple fact that telling the truth, making simple statements of fact about your identity and beliefs—particularly when they don't match up with existing social prejudices—can get people attacked, maligned, or murdered.

Photographs and
My Faux-Lesbian Body

by Emily Jenkins

T he hot summer after my freshman year in college, I posed
for some lesbian photographs.

Or maybe they weren't lesbian photographs. You tell me.

I was pretty rabidly heterosexual that June, fresh from the
ridiculous romantic escapades of my first year away from
home. I spent a lot of time indulging in melodramatic conflicts with my boyfriends, one on each coast. In the moments
left over, I worked in a Birkenstock shoe store and drank
espresso milkshakes in funky Seattle coffee shops. My friend
Ellen, an artist and photography major, asked me to pose for
some pictures.

Ellen was one of those friends you have when you are
young who seem further initiated into the mysteries of life
than you could ever be. In high school she had dated a married man and lost her virginity to a college boy long before I
had gone past second base. She had a nose ring and an older
brother with a motorcycle who would flirt with me at parties.
She was the first girl I knew to have her own apartment, and
she named her cat after Ntozake Shange. That summer, Ellen

was also my only friend who was, to my knowledge, exploring homosexuality.

When Ellen came out to me, she wasn't apologetic. She told me directly that she assumed I would accept her no matter what her sexual relationships were.

She was right. She said she was bisexual and was involved in her first lesbian relationship. She wanted her photographs to express an intimacy between two women that she was just discovering herself. The other model would be our friend Maya. Polite, preppy, and beautiful, Maya dreamed of being a doctor. She was shedding her compliant reputation in her first year away from home: the previous semester, in the heady anger that follows Introduction to Women's Studies, she had imposed a period of mutual celibacy on her boyfriend. He was waiting patiently for it to be over.

I said yes, I would pose.

Ellen's photographs would include naked and partly naked shots of me and Maya in daily activities: washing dishes, watching television, combing our hair, sleeping. In agreeing to model for them, I felt much the same way as I had when Ellen told me about her girlfriend: that here was a situation in which my better self—my accepting, open-minded, uninhibited self—was being called into action. This side of me isn't always on the surface, though I wish it were; it gets buried in my day-to-day nervous perfectionism. In asking me to pose for these photographs, Ellen offered me a chance to drop my inhibitions, to accept and celebrate both her choices and my own body.

The fleeting peacock glow of satisfied vanity I experienced in having so many pictures taken of me was almost completely overshadowed by my fear of getting naked. I was terrified of my body being judged. This was partly because, in the pictures, it was a lesbian body in contact with another. What would people think? What did I myself think? But even more overwhelming for me than masquerading as a lesbian was my painful teenage fear of being ugly or fat.

Choosing to be photographed despite those fears offered me a chance to prove they were worthless. Forcing myself to be uninhibited, both about nudity and about the sexuality implied in the images, was a liberating experience.

Just like most of the liberating experiences I'd had in my short life—an acid trip, learning to drive, learning to water-ski, crying in acting class, losing my virginity—it was also awkward and a little ridiculous. We started in the kitchen, wearing our underwear and doing housework. Isn't this a male fantasy? we wondered. Then we moved to the bathroom, where Maya dried her hair and I sat on the toilet and pretended to confide in her my deepest secrets. Later Ellen had us jump up and down naked for two whole roles of film. These shots are absurd; our breasts flop off in opposite directions and our legs dangle strangely. We were sweating in the heat and kept drying ourselves off on Ellen's bath towels.

Maya and I laughed with bravado, making jokes to ease our discomfort. We made an excess of conversation. Candy's new boyfriend, heir to a pepperoni empire, had stood her up. Alex, a skateboard punk boy we knew from hanging out in front of the record store, was playing in a band downtown. Trivial stuff. Joan Armatrading and Sade lamented from the stereo in the bedroom. I complained about looking thick and pale next to Maya's slight Japanese frame. We wondered if we looked sexy. We wondered what our boyfriends would say. Would they be appalled? Turned on? Neither of these responses was any good, so we decided not to tell them at all.

Ellen told us to shut up, we were beautiful and the light was fading, so we had to hurry. She wanted to get some shots by the window.

In these pictures—and this is true of all photographs to some extent—I look like myself and not myself. In many, I seem unrecognizable in the white camisole Ellen gave me to wear, smoking an unfamiliar cigarette in an unfamiliar kitchen. I am unrecognizable holding Maya's hand tenderly as I watch her sleep. In some pictures I see things I don't want to see: baby fat, a frown, or—in small pictures destined to remain on the contact sheet—I am cringing with shyness or tension. In others, Ellen has captured a moment that triggers a flash of self-knowledge, as in a picture of me topless, staring ambivalently at my reflection in a full-length mirror. In a few, I appear magically how I wish I could always be— natural, relaxed, beautiful, expressive.

So were they lesbian photographs? Did the pictures do what Ellen wanted them to do? Did they fully communicate her experience of lesbian relationships and her appreciation of women's bodies? Or, because the pictures were essentially faked, were they inadequate? Maybe, because both Maya and I were straight, they lacked some intangible contribution that lesbian models could have made to the images: looks of desire, a sense of ease in being naked together, something. If the models had been lovers, the tiny details of a relationship that are impossible to manufacture would somehow have been captured on film—small gestures of affection, power dynamics, shared style, shared facial expressions. On the other hand, Maya and I did have a friendship of our own. I had cheated off her calculus homework senior year in high school and been sick all over the back of her father's fancy white car one night after too much rum. We had spent hours eating cake after school at the B & O Espresso shop, where our friend Stephanie had taught us both how to give hand jobs, demonstrating the technique on a spoon. Maya and I had worked on the high school newspaper together. This friendship did form an element of Ellen's images. Perhaps it lent an intimacy to the pictures that would not have been possible if the models had been "real" lesbians but strangers to each other.

Lesbian photographers and filmmakers whose work I've seen generally avoid these problems by working with lesbian subjects. Filmmaker Rose Troche claimed in an interview that all the women in her movie were lesbians: *"Go Fish* doesn't even consider the straight world. . . . Every one you see on the screen in *Go Fish* is gay."[*] Lesbian feminist photographers like Joan E. Biren (JEB), Danita Simpson, Tee Corrinne, and Bettye Lane have focused on documenting lesbian culture through portraits, erotica, or photojournalism.[†] These artists often emphasize that theirs are photographs or films of self-identified lesbians, not actors or models; many ensure their subjects' privacy by promising to exhibit the pictures only within certain contexts, and others provide release forms that allow the subjects to approve the sorts of publications in which they might appear. Much of this emphasis on documentation is part of the ongoing objective shared by many gay artists of helping to create a culture, of making visible what was previously invisible.

But if you are not a lesbian, can you share this objective? Do Ellen's photographs of faux-lesbian bodies contribute to lesbian visibility, or do they somehow undermine it? Would the images be even less valid if the photographer herself were straight? Perhaps so, but then they'd be easier to categorize and understand. They would express an idea of lesbian relationships seen through the lens of heterosexuality.

Will this outside information affect the viewer of the photograph? Could images like Ellen's still have a genuine quality? Could they still seem "real"? Or will they reek of artifice, of something that is not quite true, not quite lesbian, which will become intelligible to the viewer only when the sexuality of the artist and her models is known?

Fake images of lesbians are a staple of the men's hetero-

---

[*] Quoted in Martha Baer, "Go Figure," *Village Voice,* June 28, 1994, p. 70.

[†] The only exception I have come across in my limited research, most of which was done at the Lesbian Herstory Archives in Brooklyn, is Kaucyila Brooke, an artist described in an article by Jan Zita Grover. Brooke employs her subjects as actors and creates tableaux that are intended to metaphorically reconstruct various relationship patterns. However, Brooke's actors are, Grover implies, all lesbians themselves. Jan Zita Grover, "Dykes in Context: Some Problems in Minority Representation," in *The Contest of Meaning: Critical Histories of Photography* (Cambridge: MIT, 1989), p. 189.

sexual pornography industry. Two girls and one guy, two girls together, two girls together in cowboy clothes, two girls together in a hot tub. The tacit premise of these images is that the women in them are not really woman-oriented. We are meant to assume that—both in real life and in the scenario of the photographs—the models' sexual interest is in men. The male viewer's presence is the key to the turn-on, for the girls in the pictures and for the viewer himself. An actual or apparent lack of interest in that male gaze would deprive the image of its heterosexual power.

While Ellen's pictures were not pornographic or explicitly sexual, pictures of two naked straight women faking lesbianism still have links to images like those I just described—images that are emphatically *not* expressions of women's sexuality or of our relationships with each other because they are constructed by and for male viewers. Perhaps, because of their artificiality, photographs like Ellen's can never be free of their tacit associations with men's pornography. Perhaps the pictures I was in contributed to the world's repertoire of exploitative images. Critics like Teresa de Lauretis, for example, have criticized lesbian erotica because the standard pornographic scenario is based on straight representational and social norms. [*]

Lesbian sexuality, even depicted through these standard scenarios, may be misunderstood by a typically straight gallery audience. When images are created that *do* challenge those norms, that audience is even less likely to comprehend them. An artist like Ellen must decide for herself who these pictures are for and where they will be displayed. Theorist Jan Zita Grover poses this problem in terms of a subculture, as she defines the lesbian community, and a dominant culture. Messages created by the subculture are incomprehensible to members of the dominant culture unless the artist

---

[*] Teresa de Lauretis, "Film and the Visible," in *How Do I Look?: Queer Film and Video,* ed. Bad Object-Choices (Seattle: Bay Press, 1991), p. 256.

makes a special effort to communicate. When Ellen displayed her photographs at her university's gallery, she had to choose whether or not to show images that would be intelligible to straight viewers, and if so, which straight viewers she wanted to reach.

As part of the dominant culture, straight artists—especially educated white people like me—do not have this problem of audience. And it is because we do not that I wonder if we have a right to do what I did: to pose as lesbians—to represent that subculture to its own members and to those outside it.

Certainly I, a straight woman with some lesbian pals, can go to Henrietta's in the West Village or read *The Advocate* without experiencing a crisis of identity. I can go to a party or two and read books on queer theory and never wonder if I have a right to do so. But when it comes to being photographed as someone I am not, I do begin to wonder. I feel like an impersonator. How can I possibly understand the lesbian position I am supposedly representing?

In posing for Ellen's portraits as if we were lesbians, Maya and I were engaging in a form of naked masquerade. Whereas cross-dressers, both male and female, put on the delicate lingerie or tailored suits typical of the other gender, we assumed another sexual orientation by taking off our clothes. In fact, not even so much in taking off our clothes as in taking them off together. It was only because Maya was in the pictures with me that I was putting on a disguise. If Ellen had photographed each of us alone, she might have created images expressive of lesbian desire for another woman's body, but the masquerade on my part would have disappeared.

The weird illegitimacy of my position as a model occurred because the masquerade was so invisible. There were no clothes to mark its presence, as there would be in cross-dressing, and no format that would alert the viewer. When we view photographs in a fashion magazine, for example, they typically depict heterosexual scenarios: men and women kiss good-bye at a train station, flirt shamelessly by the seashore, check each other out in a Paris café. Surely not all the models are straight, but the contrived lighting, glamour makeup, and editorial copy let us know these are mannequins displaying this season's new fake furs and vinyl miniskirts. When we see films or stage plays, the conventions of the drama assure us that we are watching actors playing parts. In newspaper photography, we are confident of the documentary veracity of the images. These viewing conventions disappear when we look at "art" photographs, especially portraits—we cannot be sure whether the pictures show us real people, actors, or something in between.

The question is: do these portraits, however "real" or illegitimate, affect the world outside the gallery? Is contact with the dominant culture, either by using straight models or by showing to a straight audience, a productive enterprise? Is it worth risking, as Ellen did, artistic failure and misunderstanding by audiences, gay and straight, to make visible what has been invisible?

I think it is, though my only proof comes in personal snapshots.

Photographer JEB said in 1979 that her first lesbian photograph was made because she had never seen a picture of two women kissing and she wanted to see it. "I borrowed a camera," she explains, "but I didn't even know anybody else I could ask to pose. . . . So I held the camera out at arm's length and kissed my lover, Sharon, and took the picture."[*]

I have seen two such pictures recently, yet neither of them are of lesbians. One, enlarged to twelve by fifteen inches, decorates a wall in my friend Polly's bedroom. It shows her and her closest friend kissing enthusiastically on the lips, arms wrapped around each other. The second sits in my scrapbook, and a copy of it decorates my grandmother's

---

[*] Quoted in Judith Schwartz, "Introduction," in Joan E. Biren, *Eye to Eye: Portraits of Lesbians* (Washington D.C.: Glad Hag Books, 1979), p. 10.

dressing table. It shows her, age seventy-eight, and me, age twenty-five, standing on the beach at Martha's Vineyard. We are kissing on the lips.

These photographs are incredibly joyful. In being free to physically express our love for one another and to capture those moments on film, straight women are benefiting hugely from lesbian photographers like JEB, who set out aggressively to create the images that could not be found elsewhere. However illegitimate my own appearance in such images might have been, the experience affected me positively. My continuing interest in lesbian pictures stems from a sense that photographs like the one in my scrapbook might not exist without them. The distribution of lesbian art in those very contexts where the dominant culture audience poses such a problem for the artist has begun, at least, to create what Audre Lorde termed "a lesbian imagination in all women."

Seeing images of love between women—on the street and in photo albums, photography exhibits, magazines, and movies—does not just inform straight women about lesbian lives. It has also made me, Polly, my grandmother, and other women like us less afraid. Less afraid that we might be labeled lesbians for showing our affection to one another, because the word "lesbian" does not seem insulting. Less afraid that physical contact must imply homosexuality, because homosexuality no longer needs to be implied; it can be openly expressed.

Lesbian images that are shown outside the lesbian community serve as a visual reminder to straight women that we may choose to be woman-oriented. They remind us that our central relationships may be with each other as well as with men. Working in our patriarchal offices, trying to forge equal partnerships, struggling through the everyday troubles of loving the opposite sex, we need such reminders. And we are grateful for them.

Almost a Dyke : In Search of the Perfect Bisexual

by Michelle T. Clinton

I wanted to be the perfect bisexual. I wanted to be the ideal, nonthreatening bisexual to whom political lesbians would give the honorary dyke award. I wanted to be the one who could cross the line between straight and lesbian culture and slip the secrets of the good-time women-only space into the hands of lonely, frustrated straight girls who were being cheated by men. I wanted the perfect, bizarre kind of self-deception that would be absolute proof of a soul so complex that no one, no group, could claim to understand or predict my behavior. I wanted to be mysterious and unknown: I wanted secrets, masks, mystery. Because I found perfect self-knowledge impossible. Because I believed that to give any ideology or culture an unchallenged claim on my identity was a kind of spiritual death, the end of spontaneity and surprise, the beginning of a stagnant life of predictable, empty gestures. Fuck that.

My bisexuality is part of the expression of the flexibility, the changeability of my spirit that feels essential and pre-

cious to the center of my life. My bisexuality is a part of my
desire to remain an outsider, to be able to "pass" into polar-
ized worlds, to abandon expectation, to honor the mystery of
being. My bisexuality is a celebration of the ever-opening
flesh, the expansive, fluid mirror of social discourse.

My personal story is this: I came out as a lesbian twenty
years ago. I stayed out in all situations of my life—my family, my job, my neighborhood, and so on—for the next seven
years. And though I felt happier than ever before, though I
felt that my life had direction, that my deepest self could
evolve and heal inside the lesbian community of women of
color, I had to admit that my sex life was a wreck. My erotic
relationships with women were shot through with instability,
betrayal, drama, and sexual frustration. My sexual self and
my social-political self fragmented into irreconcilable parts.
(I am a radical feminist: I have no interest in bisexual "hu-
manism.") So in an act of desperation, in a need for sexual
fulfillment, I left town and reversed the coming-out process.
I became straight again, thinking that I had never been gay at
all, that I was a straight woman who loved the companionship of women.

I found sex with men better but life with men impossible.
And when a gay woman explained to me that my difficulty
with lesbian sex was something she could help me with, I
came out again. As a bisexual. Because I finally understood
that though culturally I am woman-identified, I am erotically
attracted to both women and men.

Both the relationships I have had since then, as a bisexual
with stone butch lesbian women, sizzled with sexual power
and radiated healthy growth for both my partner and me.
Lesbians willing to love bisexuals are not uncommon. Likewise, lesbian bigots who bash and insult bisexuals are not
rare. I have been called names, stared at, shunned, given the
silent you-are-invisible treatment, screamed at, and denied
entrance to women's gatherings. (I don't try to go to lesbian-
only functions because I fully respect the need for and right

to lesbian-only space.) One woman actually gave my lover advice on how to control me (tips on dildo usage) so that I would not go back to men. I put her out my house.

And so my sense of oppression expanded to include both the wave of hateful homophobia in the culture at large and the stagnant pool of lesbian bigots who fear, distrust, hate, and consequently hurt me.

Because I wanted and needed the respect of the lesbian community, I believed that if I could keep quiet about my true sexuality and "behave" properly—being monogamous with women only, not flirting, practicing safe sex, and so on—I could then earn the respect of my community. That I could be a "good" bisexual, "practically a dyke." And that I could force the bigots to admit, as if their prejudices were justified, that there are exceptions. And that the perfect bisexuals were functionally as good as lesbians and so should receive lesbian cultural "privilege."

I am different: for most of my life I wanted desperately to be a lesbian. My body denied me that desire. Gradually I listened to the beauty of that difference; I came to look into the sphere of the unknown, the mysterious aspects of being human that are beyond control and predictability. I came to relax my thinking, my expectations, my desire for willful control of my identity.

I remember learning the lesson of being different—an outsider in the African-American community because I'm queer, an outsider in the mainstream culture because I'm a poet—how deeply painful it was, how much agony I held inside my body, when I feared the loss of the only loving community I had ever known. The day that agony lifted from me, I learned that to be different is the greatest gift possible of a unique character: that I had the potential for a true, deep life, the potential for change. The instincts inside me, the impulses I would not explain were for the good, and that somehow connected to the whole of my being. Years of experience were condensed into a voice that said, "You are different. This is not some constellation of the mind. You are concretely different, and you will never know the comfort of a family that fits around you, a community that recognizes you without a fight, a country that does not question, chastise, hurt, or exalt you. You will never be a part of a group."

As that voice became a sad strength and comfort to me, as I began to move through every social interaction without expectation of a mirror, as I moved like a stray, a guest, through every gathering of people open to me, I felt more at ease, more relaxed than ever before. Because I no longer expected people to be like me. I came to accept and celebrate the ways in which people are different. That intimacy and support and the human exchange of *chi,* warmth, food, stories, touch, need not be grounded in the same shape of culture or belief.

When I am around lesbians, which is most of the time, my identity mixes and withdraws to such an extent that I can only really describe it metaphorically: I see myself wrapped inside a membrane of uniqueness that only I am aware of. Sometimes the membrane thins to the point of complete invisibility and I am inside the crowd. A crowd of lesbians. The happiness is happening. We're all inside this newfangled radical space of pure self and collective invention, beating every intention of the white man to keep us apart, keep us fearful and dejected. We are beating every intention of the patriarchy because the potluck is fattening, the music is ethnic, the hang is multicultural. The women are seriously radiant and open, and I am the truest me that I could ever be: I don't even miss my mother, I don't long for a pro-gay black community, I don't resent the dysfunction in my biological family, because the membrane of separation has been melted by the love of lesbian women.

Other times the membrane is held fast and thick: I can't reach out. The words and gestures of support are too blunt and betray my subtlety. The women feel like bullies: they pick on and dismiss women who are different. Sometimes we cannot connect. And I fall into that easy pit of self-negation and try to force the membrane of separation to disappear. Instead of trusting that the interaction has failed for its own reasons, I assume the failure occurred because of my sexuality. I then crave a pure lesbianism for myself. I think, I'm not like the other bisexuals. I can commit to women. I'm as good as any lesbian. I'm the perfect bisexual.

Once, at a card party of African-American lesbians, I led my partner to a solid trip to Boston, which means we lost no tricks, we won the hand. We'd been losing most of the night, so I got real excited and jumped up, slapped her a high five over the table, wiggled my butt, laughed, and yelled, "Not bad for a bisexual. Right, baby?" An awkward silence spread through the room while my lover gathered up the cards and started to shuffle.

"You know you sweet. You know you smooth, girl," she told me, and winked. And I was glad for the love of a good woman, but I started to get that feeling. Like I was not welcome in woman-space, I was not welcome as a bisexual at any lesbian social hour.

"Are you really a bisexual?" one of the women asked.

I nodded.

Then the woman looked at my lover and said, "I'd watch her if I were you. You know what they say about bisexuals. You got to control them."

So we got into it. A heated group discussion about bisexuals. In general the sisters were cool. It turned out two of the other women (out of a total of eight) were bisexual too, and damn proud of it. So I had plenty of backup. During the next few hands, we talked about sexuality, change, and acceptance among women. At first I was defensive, even a little pissed off, that this was perceived as a potential problem. But after we talked, I felt better.

So I am learning that the perfection of sexuality is a myth, some impossible standard that is really about not accepting the self. I am learning to stand up for myself, to stand up for diversity, to live and work for a community of women that is open and accepting. I am learning that the truest perfection of my bisexuality is about an enrichment of "lesbian space," and that many lesbians welcome us. That the search for the perfect bisexual is a search for self-acceptance, a search for a loving community. And I am still committed to that search.

5

Blurred Boundaries, or Which One Is the Lesbian?

The Queer Kitchen

by Indigo Som

context is everything. here is mine: i was born in san fran-
cisco, a cancer in the year of the horse. my spirituality is
deeply rooted in this place, the bay area, which is my home
in every possible sense of the word, from santa cruz in the
south to point reyes and the beginning of the wine country in
the north. my parents are both architects, originally from
hong kong and canton. i grew up in marin county (one scar-
let bridge north of san francisco), an area notorious for be-
ing rich—cocaine-rich, and just as white—and attended an
exclusive, oppressive private prep school there.

i left to go to college in rhode island, where i figured out
that i was not a white male, my upper middle class economic
background notwithstanding. having made this discovery, i
returned to the bay area for art school and eventually gradu-
ated from uc berkeley in ethnic studies after five years of col-
lege in three different schools. i am a writer, an artist ("in
recovery from art school"), radical, and bisexual. i also hap-
pen to be a vegetarian (although i sometimes eat seafood &
even poultry—perhaps i should say i'm a vegetarian-identi-

fied omnivore), & environmentalist, with a strong (if not im-
mediately apparent) hippie edge. i am happiest in mixed
groups of queer women of color, especially if they are cre-
atively oriented. i have no disabilities that i know of (yet). i
dream a lot, always in color. i am in my mid-twenties, living
in the east bay for five years now and plan to stay here for a
very long time, probably forever.

Lesbians like to ask me if I am a lesbian-identified bisexual, but I refuse to identify as anything other than what/who I really am, so I call myself a bisexual-identified bisexual. (Not that different from being a woman-of-color-identified woman of color, right, sisters?) This assertion usually causes serious conceptual problems, until people can get beyond the rigid duality that hangs us up in our society: hetero-homo, male-female, good-evil, white-black. Being neither white nor black, and often invisible because of it, I learned early that this simplistic kind of categorizing system just does not work. Let's face it, folks, the world is a little more complex than that. Complex and wonderful. Of course it hasn't always been wonderful for me. For a long time I was in a sort of coming-out stagnation. Being bi was not something to be happy about; it was a problem. I only felt the oppression. I thought it would be so much easier if I were either straight or lesbian. If only I were not attracted to men, if only I didn't have such great sex with them, then I could go running into the open cozy arms of the lesbian community and live happily ever after. I never really thought that if only I didn't find women so attractive I wouldn't have a problem either; trying to be a straight feminist—a womanist,[*] actually—caused me no end of internal conflict, only some of which can be attributed to my coming-out process.

---

[*] *Womanist:* Alice Walker's term for a feminist of color, fully defined in the front of her book *In Search of Our Mothers' Gardens* (New York: Harcourt Brace Jovanovich, 1983).

So there I was—twenty, twenty-one, then twenty-two years old—and knowing the whole time that there were some incredibly fine women around whom I would love to at least kiss or hug or maybe—just maybe—undress. (I was afraid to think about what I might do once I got past the clothes. Years of living in a homophobic world can cramp your style considerably.) However, as a supposedly straight womanist, I had been in enough contact with the lesbian community to know that I would get infinitely more shit from many lesbians for being bi than I was getting from my mostly straight, feminist radical circle of friends. Actually, I got a lot of support and encouragement from my straight friends, so for a long time I couldn't see why I should bother to try getting involved in the lesbian community at all. I was very into being single and was content to have an occasional fling or one-night stand with men. Just a couple little things seemed out of place.

For one thing, and this should be obvious, I was isolated as a queer. No commonalities or validation or role models or any of that stuff that it takes to figure out what it really means to be queer. Supportive straight friends can't do all that for you. The other thing was that I was in love with a woman. Very minor detail. Both of us were in absolute, complete denial about it. I think her being haole* put me even more in denial about my feelings for her. We were incredibly close friends and always overjoyed to see each other. We sometimes flirted. I even had sexual dreams about her, but I wrote them off as random coming-out dreams having nothing really to do with her. A few times we even tried making out, laughing uproariously the whole time from sheer nervousness. Once I kissed her and she fled shrieking and giggling into the kitchen, where my lesbian housemate took one look at us and said, "Why don't you guys just go do it?" We almost died laughing.

---

* *Haole*: Hawaiian term for European white people, literally meaning "outsider" or "without land." This word seems to be creeping into common usage among mainland Asian-Americans.

This "friendship" of ours survived numerous long-distance separations while we each jumped from school to school trying to finish our undergrad degrees. I still have piles of her letters, and the phone bills are better forgotten. Eventually we both graduated. She came back to the East Bay and moved into the apartment I shared with "my other best friend," a very heterosexual Asian-American woman who was traveling in Asia at the time. Everything fell to pieces. Put into my colored context, living in my colored home, this would-be girlfriend suddenly seemed uncomfortably white to me. She was seeing a haole guy who also seemed awkwardly out of place among my friends of color. Somehow they had a stiffness, a rigidity, something missing in their humor; they had those qualities that I always associated with *other* haoles, not my friends.

I was experiencing a time-earthquake. (This earthquake-consciousness theory of mine comes from growing up in earthquake country. Things—plates of the earth, or your own personal growth—are moving past each other all the time, but you aren't aware of the movement, the change, until the edges of the plates snap past each other to produce an earthquake, and the landscape readjusts to its new reality.) While my friend was still in Rhode Island, I was in the Bay Area getting heavily into Ethnic Studies and the community of people of color around it. I had grown to expect a highly developed consciousness around issues of race and ethnicity. Haoles who didn't have that kind of understanding and commitment couldn't be my friends. This woman, my "best friend," who I used to think was the coolest white person I knew, suddenly seemed not to understand the first thing about living in a multicultural community, didn't know anything about people of color beyond theory. I asked her to move out. She did, angry at my impatience with her. We tried to talk, but didn't get anywhere.

In the fall, my housemate returned from Asia, even more off-balance about men than she had been before. Or else I was just more aware of it. She resumed her dysfunctional relationship with her arrogant alcoholic boyfriend, and they began to have awful fights. Meanwhile her self-righteously "radical" sexist brother was homeless and crashing in our living room with his girlfriend, both of them mooching our food, our toothpaste, and other life necessities. They fought constantly as well. This boundless heterosexual nightmare, not to mention my friendship with my housemate, kept deteriorating until I moved out several months later in total disgust.

In the middle of all this pain and chaos, which included a real earthquake in October, I realized that something just wasn't working. Out of sheer instinct, I think, I made a New Year's resolution to go to a support group of queer Asian women. Most of them were lesbian, but they turned out to be at least bi-friendly enough for me to feel accepted, if not completely understood. While I was getting used to being in that community, organizers were planning the first national bisexual conference for June. I joined the people of color caucus and for the first time felt that there was something really wonderful about being bisexual. Finally there were people like me! People who understood me exactly as myself instead of trying to relate to only a fragmented part of me. At last I was allowed to indulge in my bisexual point of view instead of feeling that I had to squeeze into the lesbian community's margins. The actual conference itself, although a little too white for my taste, strengthened my pride even more.

Not long afterward I fell in love for the first time in years. My lover is a wonderful Japanese-American musician who is the most bi-friendly lesbian I have ever met. She likes to tell people that it doesn't matter if she's sleeping with a lesbian or a bisexual woman, as long as it's a woman! She is attracted to a gender, not an orientation. This makes so much sense to me. I, on the other hand, am attracted to qualities other than gender, although I am not gender-blind by any means. Far from it. I appreciate different things about women and men, whether I sleep with them or not, just as I appreciate different things about different cultures: Chinese chow fun, Afro-Cuban drums, Navajo weaving. . . . I demand only integrity, a creative spirit, radical understanding, and an open-minded willingness to struggle.

Bi is beautiful! I no longer accept falsely imposed limitations from either the straight mainstream or from lesbians and gay men. I can't be monosexual any more than I can be monocultural. The lesbian and gay community needs to see that we are not a threat, that we are not confused, that we should be included as a visible part of the movement, and that such inclusion can only strengthen us all. We have always been here in the community. Bisexuals are queer too, and like all other queers, we must fight heterosexism every day of our lives. "You can't have your cake and eat it too," they tell me. Well, sure I can, if I learn to bake. Then I can not only eat cake forever, but I can have all different kinds. I can even have bread. Bisexual inclusion can only make the queer community richer and more nourishing—more powerful. My beloved sisters of color, welcome to the queer kitchen!

The Old Age Home

by Sharon Thompson

Maybe we're good friends who love each other, or maybe we're two people who used to be lovers but aren't anymore and aren't good friends either or who used to be friends but now feel like ex-lovers; and maybe he and I, we're two people who are afraid to be lovers because it would be like sleeping with our mothers. Or maybe we're all just people who used to have a lot to say to each other but haven't accepted that those things pass like everything else.

So then, the sexual questions are minor in comparison. Except that lately sex is all I think of when I see her, which I never would have expected earlier. Maybe she's desirous in general currently and I'm receptive to desirousness. (I'm saying nothing is all one-sided.) Or maybe she looks like a female version of someone who molested me when I was four, or maybe not molested but rocked me, sang me lullabies, and I've forgotten, because I really wanted him. Or her. Or didn't. Or half did and half didn't.

Or maybe wanting her is nothing more than a paraphiliacal misperception of appetite or a transformation of my irritation into something I earlier and subconsciously assumed would be nicer but which now we both understand is also more awful and dull, the intrajection of envy, as someone put it recently. And he and I, we're two people who are afraid to be lovers because it would be like sleeping with our mothers.

Or maybe we're two good people who would never have been lovers in a million years and aren't friends, either, and maybe she and I, we're two people who would like to be lovers because it would be like sleeping with our fathers, but we are old enough to know better, and that's why when I see her I feel as if I am about to be caught by the police.

Or maybe we're just two people who used to have a little to say to each other and now have nothing. But that must mean something. However you look at it, one thing is clear: we missed our chance to be lovers—although there is a lot we don't know about the future.

Or maybe I'm currently desirous in general, though I don't like to admit it, and she's receptive. Or possibly she looks like a female version of someone who loved me when I was four, and I've forgotten because I really wanted to be left alone. (After all, isn't love a form of molestation?)

I've always believed it would prove to be an algebraic matter finally, an equation in which the factors are economics, history, class, and electricity, although not in that order necessarily.

Or maybe we just sat down across from each other because there was nowhere else to sit. Possibly that's the whole basis of all my passions, although somehow I can't believe that. Of course, it might just be conditioning making me feel that even if I don't want her now, and don't even feel like I did or I might, still I must have once or felt I would have if she had or he had not.

Or maybe we're just slips clashing in the night. Or our personal fables incidentally, and that means also impersonally, include each other as points of reference. Or maybe it *is* all one-sided. Or maybe I'm him now and he's me or I'm half him and she is half him also, so that if we got together we'd be all him and half her and half me but without his money, which is how it used to be before in a different kind of a way, and maybe I miss that, although I doubt it.

So often we are understood in the first place. First impressions? But those things pass, and we are left with the dice, the roll, the numbers come up differently every time, did you ever notice? Some settle, some don't. It doesn't matter.

I saw an old woman in the dentist's office yesterday: high cheekbones, clear eyes, tall and slender; the sort of woman who never shirks her duty or her image, keeps her pride at high shine. Her posture seemed out of character, and it frightened me. She leaned sideways in the green chair, her shoulders bent forward, her elbows on its arm, her aching jaw cupped in her hands. When the hygienist passed she straightened for a moment but soon faded back into herself, raising one pale, spotted, long-fingered hand and beginning to rub it with the other, absently, as if there were no one else in the world with whom she was in congress, except her pain; yet she was still exquisite, a sole, fragile Meissen figure.

I believe we will all be alone in the end or near the end. Children or no children, mates or no mates. Passionate friends and enemies. And this is my idea for an old age home. We forget all this and we pool our Social Security and our IRAs, and we hire anyone who is willing to scratch our heads? Rub us when they read, ruffle our fur, stroke us? Tease us? Put us away when even pain has lost its savor?

Sharing the Bathroom

by Louise Rafkin and Bárbara Selfridge

One January Louise and I both taught at Hampshire College, and every evening we disappeared for a couple of hours into the upstairs bathroom. The woman sharing the house with us would come to the bathroom door with phone messages—"I didn't know if you were here or not," she'd say, "Come in!" we'd say—and you could tell she was trying to figure out the nature of that intimacy: Louise in the tub naked, me on the toilet with my pants down around my ankles.

That housemate wanted to see our sexuality in the scene—Louise's out lesbianism, my piss-or-get-off-the-pot bisexuality—but Louise and I saw only each other's peculiarity: I accepted Louise's odd attachment to nightly baths, she accepted my slightly paranoid penchant for accident-proof seating.

We laughed at our housemate's analysis; Louise and I kept talking.

It is hard to remember when exactly Bárbara became my

friend and not just someone I worked with. It's like when you catch a cold: first you don't know you have it and then all of a sudden you can't remember ever not having it. I can't remember not having complete closeness with her, the kind where you can call up in tears, or where you can say "I need to spend the night" because you really don't want to go home that late alone and besides you know if you spend the night you'll take a bath, she'll talk to you from her seat on the toilet, and then later you'll solve cryptic crossword puzzles.

Actually, Bárbara will do most of the crosswords because cryptics are still like a foreign language to me, but I'll always get one answer she can't, so I don't get discouraged.

The first time I went to Louise's house, we were going to go to a reading, and I knocked at the sliding glass door. "Hello?" I called. "Louise?"

Louise called back—"Is that you, Bárbara?"—and when I said it was, she emerged from the stage-right bathroom, naked but semi-toweled, and scurried over to unlock the door before scurrying off to the stage-left bedroom.

Scurrying ahead of her were Louise's breasts: big, round, and perfectly aimed, sort of like rocket heads, or at least like the concentric-circle rocket bras of the 1950s, and I was homo-ignoramus enough to wonder if having breasts like that automatically made you a lesbian. Or conversely, if being a lesbian gave you breasts like that.

I'm happy to report that I came to my senses even before a dressed Louise came out of the bedroom. Breasts like that came from Louise's karate fighting, not her sexuality.

Silly me.

Our friendship started at that weird time when friendships between lesbians and straight women were strained. I spent a lot of time defacing billboards, never thinking to invite Bárbara, which I later learned made her jealous. Plus Bárbara had already had a couple of weird alliances with lesbians, so

I didn't think our friendship had much to go on. But then once we got to know each other it seemed all that was different about us was this sexuality thing, and even that wasn't so different because, as it turned out, Bárbara had come out, and still came out from time to time (because of her political comradeship with lesbians and her bucking the assumption of compulsory heterosexuality), and besides I had a crush on her best friend—who happened to be a married man.

I flirted with this man for years, and Babs even brought him to my readings, one of which was held at Red Dora's Bearded Lady and attended by the mostly young pierced and tattooed crowd. Jean-Michel seemed more interested than Bárbara and I were in keeping everyone's sexuality defined. When he found out that I'd had an affair with a man well after coming out and sometime within the first two years of us flirting, Jean-Michel got nervous. The safety net—what's the harm in a married man flirting with a lesbian?—suddenly disappeared.

Louise and I worked at a newspaper, doing paste-up, and she didn't need to tell us she was a lesbian—and we were probably too "polite" to assume it—but then she won an award for the column she wrote for the local lesbian rag, and she did have to tell us that.

Louise pressured the other newspaper she worked for into hiring me, too. That shop was union and a strange mix of men hitting on me and women who wanted to know my sexuality. (Maybe unlike the men, the lesbians were too polite to hit on me without knowing, I thought.)

Liz said, "So, Bárbara, you're married, right?"

And you know how it is when you're a sexual anorexic, totally absorbed in your own nonexistent sex life, busy trying to categorize and blame all its past and potential members, and then someone asks you that kind of question. I respected Liz's desire to know, but I couldn't answer.

"No," I said, "but you think I should be, huh?"

Mostly Bárbara and I hate our bodies, and that takes up a lot of space in our friendship. But to counter this self-hate, she persuades me to make up affirmations. ("The reason we know affirmations work," Bárbara says, "is that we can see how effective they are when we repeat the negative ones.")
"Start with your name, like this," she says. "I, Louise Rafkin, have a healthy body which is capable of giving and receiving love."

"Yeah, but I'm still fat," I say, standing naked in front of her mirror trying on everything in her closet in my search for something to wear when I give a reading.
"Look here!" I point to my hips. The problem, and Bárbara knows it, is that I'm only skinny when I'm on the Misery Diet, after a breakup or an unrequited love obsession. Sometimes, despite our affirmations, our bodies seem merely vessels for other people's love or judgments. When I get love I balloon up. Bárbara only slims down around men who prefer big women.
Bárbara rolls her eyes at me from atop her Exercycle. Perry Mason is on and I'm not supposed to talk with her during this sacred hour. Her current lovebird is nestled in the hollow of her collarbone.

Louise and I talk about lots of stuff: our shared work (paste-up), our shared vocation (writing), and our strategies for finding financial security in either; family members with drug and co-dependency addictions and how that fucks you up. How to improve our body self-images, a conversation that only slightly tempers that other conversation about how to improve our actual bodies. How to practice safe love.

We talk a lot about flirting and fighting, and we make good confidantes, maybe because we're both so interested, maybe because neither of us is rich: I have all that heterosexual privilege but give myself no permission to have affairs and take advantage of it; Louise throws herself at the feet of her love affairs, but she never gets the financial and spiritual—"You've done the right thing, dear"—rewards either. We don't envy each other, but we don't pity each other, either. There's respect between us.

I don't know what it would have been like to have a sister, especially an older sister, but sometimes that is what Bárbara feels like. Instead of a sister thing, though, we have this deal called "spousal support," which means that we trade help doing certain tasks that we really can't face doing "single." Sometimes it's about help with chores or two-person tasks; sometimes it's emotional, like making a hard phone call to an ex-lover.

I think, even after ten years, I am one of Bárbara's new friends, and I'm always aware of this. I know her other friends by name, and I know a bit about their dramas because Bárbara has this great way of helping you figure out something in your life by telling you how somebody else did it.

There was a time when Louise got hooked on dancing the two-step, and she dragged everyone she knew to a gay and lesbian dance hall called Rawhide. I went and was struck by how nice everyone looked in their nondiversity. With the exception of the one couple we named the man-boy love society, people seemed to be dancing with their mirror images: same gender, same height, same size, same age.

How right those couples all looked slow-slow-quick-quicking together, but then how scary it was during the dance lesson when the teacher told us to change partners, and I'd be squealing at the two indistinguishable men next to us: "I need the one who can lead!"

The teacher liked us, and whenever we showed up he'd announce it was a lesbian-only class and he'd threaten the male "lesbians" with an impending hands-on check of their lesbian "credentials." They laughed, we laughed, and one night I dreamed I was sharing a bed with Louise and Liz and two other lesbians from work, when I noticed a small group sitting with their backs against the wall opposite the bed.

They were sociologists—the teaching assistant and three or four students—there to study Lesbian Sexual Practices, and I was embarrassed. "I'm not actually a lesbian," I admitted. "I'm afraid I'm going to throw off your study."

"Oh, we know that," the male TA reassured me. "It makes it more interesting for us."

Bárbara's friend Jean-Michel and I finally lost our attraction for each other when we finally went out by ourselves, without Bárbara. I realized it was something about her love for both of us that kept energy in the flirtation. Alone, we were just a dyke and a straight guy being awkward with each other. With Bárbara around, we are daring and edgy, and I think each of us feels we could transcend the limitations on our lives.

Babs's analysis: "I think you were also both terrified by the incidence of date kiss."

She was referring to the fact that Jean-Michel actually kissed me—on the lips, no tongue—and I did not actually consent. Bárbara called it date kiss, like date rape, but I defended Jean-Michel.

"I went to give him one of those lesbian good-bye hugs," I told her. "It was a cultural misunderstanding."

Louise writes a column called "What's Going Down?" for a lesbian and gay newspaper I don't always see. They made her stop writing about the Rawhide because the owner was in a nasty fight with the editor, but I hear Louise regularly plugs me in print: my anti–George Bush chain letter, my proposal for an umbrella category for straights in the Lesbian and Gay Freedom Day Parade: "Co-Gays."

There was a time, right after I published a book about mothers of lesbians, when my life was full of "lesbian appearances," and Bárbara would sometimes accompany me to

*these. Too young to be my mother, too old to be a teenage les-
bian, she would often be mistaken for my lover.*

*In New York, Bárbara met me at the hotel the night before
a taping of* Geraldo. *She was with her friend Don—they'd
been waiting in the lobby, making up an Elvis-based punctu-
ation and grammar test for Don's students—and the three of
us checked into my hotel room together, though Don didn't
plan on staying. The room was small, and when we saw the
one king-sized bed, we laughed. But neither the clerk nor the
bellhop had seemed surprised at putting the three of us in
one bed.*

*When asked later, the clerk told us she'd "seen just about
every configuration possible check into that* Geraldo *room.
Two ladies and a man? I don't even blink."*

So I'm not very bisexual (no more than a couple of "lesbian
encounters"), and I was awfully surprised when, after years
of us being friends, one of Louise's confidences revealed a
lack of cunnilingus between her and her current true love—
the existence of *unexpected* cunnilingus being the exception
that proved the rule.

"You mean cunnilingus is a *choice*, that it wasn't just homophobia that made me not want to go down on those
women?" I demanded.

"Oh, honey," Louise said.

*It's when I'm with Bárbara that the delineation between
straight and gay seems most bizarre; a harsh labeling that
sorts us in ways that we shouldn't or perhaps needn't always
be divided.*

"Don't expect a pithy final quote from me," says Babs.

*But I do. I hope Bárbara and I go on forever, being friends
and confidantes and shedding pith on each other's lives.*

Low Cut

by Lisa Palac

I met Cheryl through an ad in the newspaper. It said something like "Very attractive blonde looking for female playmate. Boyfriend wants to watch." Yeah, my boyfriend wanted to watch, too.

The first time I tried answering a personal ad looking for a blue moon girlfriend, I was single and I didn't have very good luck. I wrote a short letter giving my name and phone number, and I enclosed a picture. It was one of those black-and-white photo-booth prints of me dressed in black, smiling. I hand-colored it, made it kind of arty. I never got a response. Maybe she chickened out. Maybe she thought I was a dork. I tried again with a different ad and ended up meeting this softball chick in a sports bar. I knew it would never work. I hated sports. Plus, she had bad skin.

After I started seeing Greg, I decided to try it again. Greg was the first guy I ever watched a porn movie with, and every one we rented was a lesbian one. He was an all-girl action connoisseur. He never picked a tape that had any guys in it, and I can't say I minded. Women turned me on, and besides, who wanted to see a bunch of ugly guys with nothing going on but big dicks? One night, after a sweaty session in front of the VCR, he said, "I'd like to see you do it with another woman."

Now, some women might interpret such a fantasy as the product of a selfish macho mind doped up on too much fake lesbian porno. But I thought of it more as classic bedrock eroticism. I know that watching two women fuck each other is no doubt the number one hetero male fantasy, but I like it, too. Before Greg had his bright idea, I'd slept with one woman, and it was a lot less gymnastic than any porn video. I was amazed by how soft her skin was; it really was like silk. While we were doing it, I kept thinking, Girls are so soft. Do I feel that soft to her? I was drowning in her silky water. I liked feeling her nipples in my mouth, the way her cunt smelled. Her body was peculiar and familiar at the same time. And I liked the challenge of figuring out how to hold it in my hands and make it work, how to make her come, even though I spent hours toying with my own circuitry. Greg's interest was a green light for me; he encouraged my desires. So rather than accuse my boyfriend of having a sick Bruce Seven–induced fantasy, I decided to live it out.

Finding a woman who will go home with you and your boyfriend, who, depending on the angle, looks like either Jeff Goldblum or a demented rabbit, isn't the easiest thing in the world. It's not like in the movies, where everyone just wants to fuck and suck at the drop of a hat. Greg and I spent a lot of time in bars saying, "She's cute" or "How about her?" but that's as far as it got. I got restless waiting for that perfect pickup moment, when she'd start rubbing my thigh and I'd let her mess up my lipstick while Greg silently paid the tab and guided us to his apartment. Deep down we were both nervous, and neither one of us had the courage to act.

So I wrote another letter. I picked an ad where having sex was clearly the goal. I laid it on thick this time, but didn't

send a photo. I hated giving away good pictures of myself
that I never got back. A few days later, Cheryl called. She had
this cigarette-smoking tough girl voice, but it was sexy, and
she was very matter-of-fact. She was young, early twenties,
same as me, and she gave me a detailed physical description
of herself—height, weight, bra size, always emphasizing
"very attractive"—and let me know that my fucking her "old
man" was out of the question and she wouldn't lay a hand on
mine. We arranged to meet at my favorite snotty art bar, the
New French Café. "You'll know me because I'll be wearing
a black jumpsuit," she said. Jumpsuit. My heart sank a bit.
The only place you could get a jumpsuit was at the army sur-
plus or Frederick's of Hollywood. I imagined her to look like
one of the go-go dancers on *Laugh-In:* big hair-sprayed curls
and mondo cleavage stuffed into a low-cut bell-bottom spandex capsule.

I wore black too: leather jacket, dark sweater, jeans. And I
think my hair was black then, fashionably unbrushed and
matted with gobs of gel. Greg showed up in his usual plaid
flannel shirt over some rock T-shirt, which may have been
"The Cramps: Can Your Pussy Do the Dog?" his long dark
hair equally shocked with styling goo. He had "I can't believe you're doing this" pasted on his face. I ordered a glass
of Côte du Rhône, he had Scotch. It was a late afternoon in
winter, still light out. I usually tried to wake up before the sun
went down again.

I picked Cheryl like a cherry when she walked in. Cleavage and everything, just as I'd pictured her. And she was very
attractive in a working-class way. Her sexy outfit was expected but sincere. She wore dark eye shadow and bright
pink lipstick. I watched heads turn, not because she was that
beautiful but because nobody would come to the New
French dressed like that. When she sat down, I wanted to
reach over and touch her downy, powder-puff skin. Her man,
on the other hand, was a greaseball. He had a bad haircut and
a big gut and a mustache. I can't remember his name. I was

very thankful for the anti-cockswap arrangement.

Just as she had on the phone, Cheryl got right down to business. She basically said that she and John, let's call him, answered a lot of ads and were always looking for new thrills. She wanted the four of us to go out to dinner one night to "get to know each other," and then we'd go back to their house and do it. Greg suggested he bring along something from his girl-girl collection. "But he don't touch me and you don't touch him," she reiterated. Thank God.

She dictated a very particular dress code: "I want you to wear something on top that's tight and really low cut and a miniskirt with thigh-high spike-heeled boots. Stockings and a garter belt, of course." Uh, okay. I didn't own any of these items, except the miniskirt, but I didn't want to tell her that. While Cheryl was dressing me up like a total slut, the guys were talking and snorting, bonding in that guy way. I think they were talking about beer. We made plans for the following Sunday.

The next night I got a call from Cheryl asking if I'd like to come over to their house and spend some time getting to know each other, as she put it. I said okay, but told her that Greg was working and so I wasn't gonna *do* anything, if that was what she had in mind, without him there. They picked me up and we drove to their suburban Minneapolis home. In the car I noticed that Cheryl was wearing pantyhose—not cotton tights or colored stockings, but these No Nonsense suntan-colored pantyhose. The dinosaur of hosiery. I felt bad mentally picking on her pantyhose, but they were so strangely out of date. I began to wonder if I could really *get to know* a person who wore beige pantyhose.

Their house was tiny, with paneling in the living room and a lime-green shag carpet. I sat down at the kitchen table in a chair with a wrought-iron back and puffy flowered vinyl on the seats. John handed me a Schlitz. He asked me what I did for a living. "I'm in film school," I said. He worked in a factory, I think. Then Cheryl wanted to show me some of the other responses she'd gotten to her ad.

She and I went into the bedroom, and she plopped a big cardboard box on the bed. One by one she showed me photos and letters from the girls who wanted to play with her. It had never even dawned on me to send a naked picture of myself, much less one with my legs spread wide and a dildo in my pussy. I was shocked, simply shocked, that people would send this hard-core, possibly incriminating stuff through the mail to some stranger at a P.O. box. No wonder I didn't get lucky the first time around. The letters were just as explicit, outlining how much they loved to eat pussy or how they wouldn't do anal, and of course how disease-free and "very attractive" they were. Well, who's going to admit their unattractive piggishness, right?

As we were looking through the stuff, Cheryl started rubbing my leg. Her skirt was hiking up her thighs, and I now saw that she was not, in fact, wearing pantyhose but flesh-colored nylons and an industrial-strength garter belt. I couldn't decide if that was better or worse than the pantyhose. When she saw me looking at her legs, she leaned over and kissed me. Her mouth was soft, and I liked the way she kissed. Then out of nowhere, greasy John appeared in the doorway, hand on his crotch. I gotta go, I said. She reminded me about the clothing requirements for our date. I admitted that I didn't have any thigh-high boots, so she made me try on several pairs of hers. I hoped for black, but the only ones that fit were an ugly tan with a thick brown heel. It was hard to feel sexy in tan boots, but I reminded myself to be open to new experiences.

A few days later I got another call from Cheryl. She wanted to take me lingerie shopping. Immediately I flashed on one of those contrived *Penthouse*-type letters where two innocent girls are seduced in the dressing room of the bra department by some horny saleslady. But I did need that stocking-and-garter-belt getup, so I agreed to join her.

We ended up at a suburban mall, but neither Cheryl nor any of the salespeople seemed the least bit interested in attacking me. In fact, Cheryl seemed quite nonplussed about the whole thing. She didn't even ogle as my naked breasts slipped from bra to bustier. She sat on a tiny stool outside the dressing room, dryly indicating her preferences. I picked out a lacy white set. "Now remember," she said, "always put the stockings and garter belt on first, then the panties. That way you can take the panties off without having to undo everything." On the way home she told me how she occasionally worked as a stripper, both in clubs and at bachelor parties, and about some of the other personal ad experiences she'd had. "But you know, I'm really just looking for a friend," she said. "Someone I can hang out and do stuff with, like go bowling."

The Sunday of our sordid affair finally arrived. I spent the afternoon getting dolled up in my new clothes. I piled on the eyeliner and made my hair really big with lots of spray. I remembered to put the panties on over the garter belt and tried to get as much cleavage going as possible. Ah, the boots. Now I was painted. I felt like an actor in an absurd and darkly erotic theatrical performance. My prior meetings with Cheryl had been the rehearsals for opening night. And while the meticulously premeditated sex scene gave me a sense of what to expect, it also sliced off bits of spontaneity. I wondered if I might feel the same calculated degree of excitement if we'd picked up a woman in a bar.

Cheryl and John picked us up at my place in the early evening. The deal was that Cheryl would pick a place to have dinner. I assumed it would be someplace nice and, most important, dark and mood-setting. Instead, we ended up at a family restaurant, a Denny's knockoff, right at the highway exit. It was blindingly bright, with glowing orange booths and plenty of screaming children. The place didn't even have a liquor license. I teetered through the door in my high-heeled boots looking like a Hollywood whore, feeling the burn of a thousand eyeballs. I wanted to explain to every single patron that, hey, I don't usually look like this, but that would have been impractical. The waitress sneered at us, and I knew she was thinking, Hookers. Dinner couldn't be over fast enough.

Back at their house, I finally started to unwind with a few slugs off of a Schlitz. John rolled a joint while Greg fiddled with the VCR, cueing up his favorite vibrator scene. Then the doorbell rang. Cheryl put her eye to the peephole and screamed, "Oh, shit, it's my dad!" She waved her arms insanely at John, indicating he should hide the pot and mouthed, "Turn that fucking thing off!" to Greg. "Hi, Daddy," I heard her say, sweet as pie, when she opened the door. Daddy had come, tool set in hand, to fix something. Cheryl gave him a quick kiss on the cheek, then made a few frantic introductions.

"So how do you know Cheryl?" her father asked me. My mouth hung open for about ten years, until Cheryl made up some lie. Bowling. Or maybe it was a party. "Well, seeing as you have company, I guess I'll come back tomorrow to fix that thing," he said. Oh, no, stay, I thought. Stay for a porno movie and watch your little girl get banged! I held my breath until he left.

I don't remember how long it took for everyone's edginess to dissolve, but eventually Cheryl and I ended up in the middle of the living room floor on a blanket in our underwear. Greg and John sat quietly on opposite ends of the sofa, watching. We made out for a while, slowly peeling off each other's bras. With the new panty trick I'd learned, the stockings and garter belt stayed in place. Although I actually tried to take my stockings off at one point because they started bagging at the knee and I thought it looked rather unappealing. "Keep them on," Cheryl whispered in my ear.

Exactly how I licked and sucked her or what she did to me is a melted-down dream, except for this: She brought out a strap-on dildo and told me to use it on her. It was a slender pink rubber cock attached to two white elastic straps. The dildo itself was hollow and looked oddly medicinal. (It wasn't until much later that I learned it was really a penis-extender, designed so a man could slip his cock inside of it and make himself "bigger." Makes me kinda wonder about John.)

I didn't want my naïveté to show, so I stuck my legs through the straps and Cheryl got on all fours. Just as I was getting the hang of it—I mean it's not easy to maneuver a piece of plastic that's belted to your crotch with a couple of rubber bands—one of the straps snapped.

"Oh, that happens all the time," John said and held out his hand in an offer to fix it.

I didn't have a mind-blowing orgasm. I don't think Cheryl did, either. We just stopped, I think, when Cheryl detected a feeble moan from John. Strangely enough, neither one of the guys took out their cocks and beat off during the show. Etiquette, perhaps. John didn't whip it out, so Greg decided he wouldn't either. Although in the end, John did have a large wet spot on the front of his jeans and had obviously been doing some discreet grinding.

Our good-byes were polite. I expected to have trouble tearing myself away from such a landmark moment, but what I really wanted was to be alone with Greg. We called a cab and went home.

I didn't hear from Cheryl the next day or the next week or in the following months. After all that, the pornographic reality just folded up into an odd and not particularly sexy memory. Occasionally I'd find a snapshot from the event floating in the front of my brain and I'd say to Greg, "Remember when her dad came over?" or "I can't believe that dildo broke."

Nine months later I went to interview my first porn star, Bunny Bleu, for my cut-and-paste Xerox sex zine, *Magnet School*. I walked into the adult bookstore on Hennepin Avenue and through the crowd saw Bunny having her picture taken with a fan. She and another woman were standing with their backs to the camera, arms around each other's shoulders. "Okay, on the count of three turn your heads around and smile!" said the Polaroid photographer. When the flash went off, Bunny turned and smiled and so did Cheryl. Then Cheryl turned completely around, and I saw that she was *very* pregnant.

She waddled over to me and gave me a hug. "I'm just here takin' a picture for John because he's in jail," she said. DWI. He cracked up the car really bad, but he's OK. Baby's due in a few weeks. You're doing a sex magazine, huh? Send me a copy when it's finished.

Her world was so unlike mine. The pantyhose we wore, the kitchen chairs we sat on, the liquor we drank, the way she said "old man" and I said "boyfriend," the places we hung out, all screamed class difference. I didn't feel superior or inferior, I only felt the difference. We had nothing in common except one thing: the desire for sexual adventure. Sometimes that's enough.

6

Visibility, Community, and Our Separate Spheres

Interview with Jessica Hagedorn

by Meg Daly

Q. You are a straight woman who has written lesbian characters, both in screenplay form and in fiction. What informs these characters?

A. I believe that serious writers have the ability, the itch, the
responsibility to write from many different points of
view. My job is to approach lesbian characters as I would
any other character in my stories, making sure they are
complex, interesting people. When characters are complicated, surprising, and interesting, they work for the
reader. If I can imagine being a bank teller, a whore, a
Vietnam vet, a single mother, a child, a serial killer, a
computer hacker, a prep-school slut, or a pious working-
class saint, then I can imagine being a lesbian character.
The process of developing a character involves more than
sexual identity. Even if it's the driving force, it's still only
a part of the whole picture. When I was writing the
screenplay for *Fresh Kill,* I had to ask myself numerous
other equally relevant questions besides my characters'
sexual choices: questions about ethnicity, race, class,

emotional makeup, privilege, religion, et cetera. "Straight" and "gay," "Asian-American," "minority," whatever—for me these tags are extremely frustrating. While these labels may be politically necessary, they also imply that our identities as human beings are somehow *fixed*. How boring! How limiting! How nearsighted!

Q. In other interviews you've talked about sexual identity as a part of multiculturalism. What role does lesbianism play in your claiming a multicultural identity?

A. As a woman of color and as an artist, I have chosen to live a certain kind of life. Gay people, queers, lesbians— whatever the terminology might be—are not marginal to my world. They are colleagues and peers, kindred spirits, my family, my friends, my lovers, and my collaborators. For me it's not simply a political allegiance; it's quite personal. How can I claim to be multicultural and diverse if I don't recognize and celebrate this allegiance?

There's a connection to be made with my growing up in the Philippines—a very complex, very Catholic, very macho society run by very strong women. Does that make sense? Historians have said that before the Spaniards colonized us, we were a matriarchal society. Nowadays you might find that the outspoken, educated, contemporary Filipino woman still seems to play by traditional rules. Marriage and family come first. As far as homosexuals go, the men are allowed to play certain accepted roles. They're the fools and the jesters—the dress designers, the hairdressers, the flamboyant drag queen entertainers. If they can stick by those rigid social rules and not stray from their lowly place, then they are tolerated. But for women to break taboos is a different story. Women who are lesbian are truly threatening. What role are they supposed to play in this macho society? You know what they were called there in my childhood? "Tomboys."

Q. There's not a word for *lesbian*?

A. Not in the vernacular. Women who dared to transgress in such a way were ostracized, shunned, vilified, and feared. Especially if they were butch. A certain kind of weird power was attributed to lesbians—maybe because they were women. Maybe because there was no "fool" role for them to play, no drag-queen equivalent. I'm talking about my childhood in the 1950s. I hope that by now some things have changed for the better.

I am the mother of daughters, so I don't want to make the same mistakes in teaching them how to perceive differences in people and in themselves. Though we're living in a different, seemingly more permissive urban landscape, the fact is that many people are still homophobic and ignorant, and my children are profoundly affected by their peers and by daily media bombardments. My older daughter has confronted some of my friends with *that question:* "Are you a lesbian?" I tell my friends to be honest with her. It's probably more of a question for her when my female friends are involved; gay men aren't as threatening or intriguing. It's a growing process for me, too.

Q. Do you have a sense of how Filipino-American gay people are perceived? What are their struggles? What are their lives like in the United States?

A. I think many of them feel more liberated in America. In this country you can be anonymous, you can reinvent yourself. The Filipino-Americans I know who are gay are outspoken and politically active. There seems to be an openness about working together with community activists on other pressing social issues that affect all Filipinos; this kind of camaraderie may not be so prevalent back home. There is a sense here, especially in cities like San Francisco and New York, that you are somewhat protected by the law. You can speak up just a little bit louder. Fight for your rights. Whereas back home, shame is a huge force. No matter how progressive you think you are, the country is small, Manila is even smaller, and everybody knows everybody. There is family to consider and to protect—no one wants their dirty laundry aired.

Q. Have conflicts around sexual orientation ever come up between you and your lesbian friends? Do you ever find similarities when you discuss your romantic relationships?

A. Yes to both questions.

One thing that is different between us is the issue of having to live behind a mask, having to shut up and pretend. Like my friends who have to work in really straight jobs—as teachers, for example. They have to play games, be holier than the Blessed Virgin. It's like a daily Uncle Tom act. You learn to live with it—you get really good at disguises and "beards"—but in the end it kills you. In this society, as a so-called straight woman, I have privilege. And I've had to rethink my privilege over and over again. The way I perceive it, I'm just an ordinary arty New Yorker: I have very short hair, I usually wear black pants or leggings and my de rigueur black Doc Martens. These are outward signs, fashion codes interpreted in different ways by different people. *Surface.* No big deal the way I see it—boring and normal. But then my complacency is jarred by some ugly incident—like when I walk down the street without my children in tow. This has happened to me several times, and to other women I know—harassment and verbal abuse by horny truck drivers and angry teenagers in cars with Jersey license plates. These guys are scary clichés, but they exist.

Q. Have you ever had a lesbian friend make a pass at you?

A. Interestingly enough, the women who've come on to me openly have all been bisexual. Not to say that I haven't felt an attraction from lesbian friends . . .

Q. Would you acknowledge or even be aware of that sort of attraction going on with a straight female friend? Does the fact that a friend is a lesbian give permission for that attraction to be happening?

A. I think it's a little of both. I think there are moments of attraction between straight friends—and yes, I think there
is a little more permission to explore this feeling with lesbian friends. But if you'll forgive my perverse Catholic
phrasing, political correctness works in mysterious ways.
You put this wall up because you don't want your lesbian
friends to think you're using them . . . you know, that
cliché about a straight woman having an adventure? Nobody wants to hurt anyone else; nobody wants to get her
feelings hurt.

So we're all really careful.

But maybe we should get our feelings hurt once in a
while. Risk something. How can we grow as people if we
live with such caution and anxiety? We're becoming hu-
morless and overinformed, afraid to act. So *nothing happens.*

The (Fe)male Gaze

by Elizabeth Wurtzel

Sometime during the first Indigo Girls concert I'd ever attended, at the Beacon Theater in 1990, my friend Daphne leaned over and whispered in my ear between songs. "You know," she said, gesturing toward the two women on stage, "they just *have* to be lesbians. They could never *not* be. I mean, they could never be anything else. Do you know what I'm saying?"

I knew exactly what she meant. And this had nothing to do with the politics of outing or anything like that, because it was well known among fans—and quietly admitted even by the people at Epic, the Girls' record label—that both Amy Ray and Emily Saliers were gay. More so than the many other singer-songwriters who were presumed, correctly or not, to be lesbians over the years, the Indigo Girls were the most tacitly open about their gay identity long before they made an official announcement in 1993 confirming everyone's suspicion. That was the year, amid post-inaugural fever in the aftermath of the Reagan-Bush era, that k.d. lang,

Melissa Etheridge, and Janis Ian also saw fit to come out with it. But what Daphne observed at the concert that night was an aesthetic approach that the Indigo Girls had—both to their music and to their presentation—that simply *had* to be the stuff of lesbianism. And I don't mean that in the usual stereotypical ways: I don't mean that they had dykey layered haircuts (though they did) or that their physical presence was boxy and mannish (though it was) or even that their intermittent chatter was laced with references to Sapphic icons like Virginia Woolf and Audre Lorde and Radclyffe Hall (it wasn't). It was more a total quality that emanated from that stage, a full-bodied and even excessive expression of unshackled emotionalism, of unfettered need and shameless want—this concert was a song cycle of liberation—that could only be a product of a world of, to paraphrase Hemingway, women without men. There was something about the Indigo Girls' music, and particularly their live performances, that just had to be the result of divorcing one's mind and one's sexual concerns from the opinion—perhaps even the gaze—of men.

The *male gaze:* the eye of Big Brother that observes, watches, possibly even censors every act we commit, every bit of art we create. It informs us even when it isn't there, because it is built into our heads and hearts, it is the collective unconscious, it is the honor system within. When I was in college, it was quite fashionable to write literary criticism papers about the male gaze, to turn it into a thesis topic, to point out how female art could be undermined by or become a trenchant challenge to the primacy of male vision. But it was all about theory, all about academic fashion and gender studies and the germinal phases of the politically correct movement. That any attempts to break free of that male gaze—that deeply penetrating glance—were almost impossible for any woman who was still attracted to, dating, sleeping with, living with, or married to a man was not something that feminist theory could readily deal with. The idea was always that if you could recognize it and criticize it, you could also, so to speak, *disappear* it.

As if understanding thunderstorms could make them stop.

Heterosexual women live in a world of male pleasure, and despite our complaints, I must assume we like it like that. At the very least, I do. I like wearing high heels, and it's not because they make my feet feel good. When spring turns to summer and it's time to wear pumps without pantyhose and I get blisters on my toes and heels from friction and leather, I feel absurdly and obscenely delighted in the shackles of womanhood that cause this unnecessary pain, this silly Occidental version of foot-binding that is really just a variation on soul-binding. I like being bound, amid all my radical feminism, to what boys want.

And yet I envy the Indigo Girls their freedom. But before I explain what I mean by freedom, which is a massive and overused abstraction, especially in what is known as the free world, I need to explain my theory of tears. Because what this is really all about is the freedom to cry, and to do it in a certain voice, in a voice that—pardon the mixed metaphor— is beyond the male gaze.

I remember being happily surprised as a college freshman when a classics professor (the classics, after all, were at the time being used by the likes of Allan Bloom to celebrate the frankly homoerotic Platonic ideals that all but hung a shingle on the gates of the canon and outside the walls of academia that might as well have read "No Girls Allowed") referred to Carol Gilligan's book *In a Different Voice* to talk about the use of hired female mourners to cry at ancient Greek funeral rites. His point was convoluted, something about the frequent need, in Hellenic culture, to employ a chorus of female stand-ins to express the sorrow and overwhelming grief that could not be spoken by men. But the professor's larger point was about the language created by all people on the margins, the peculiar dialects that are trafficked in by all outsiders, whether it's Black English, New York Jewish idiom, or just plain old girl talk. And while these alternative social groups must learn how to speak not only their own language but also the standard tongue of the dominant class—in other words, that of white men—mainstream culture has no need to return the favor. As a result, millions of Americans speak White Male as well as some version of a secondary Pidgin English, but the native speakers of White Male never cross the line and learn Alternativespeak.

And just as we as women have learned, coyly or wisely, and over aeons of evolutionary progress, how to translate our particular language into terms that men will understand, how to cross the border from Herspace to Everyspace, we have done the same thing with our emotions. We have become clever manipulators, deft interpreters, subconsciously incorporating all the proper signposts into our gusts and gestures so that we don't have to spend our lives screaming, *"This is how it feels."* We cry to men, we cry beautiful, luxuriant, elegant tears to men, we appeal to their soft spots, we appeal to their hard-ons, we flood over with tears when we are sad, we let them see our fear, our weakness, and our trust in their masculine strength, a trust that allows us to fall apart in their arms, to leak copious tears. We cry gently, meekly, sweetly, childishly, babyishly: we retreat to girlhood in our energetic release. Bob Dylan, as usual, got it absolutely right when he wrote, about some anonymous "she" (Edie Sedgwick? Joni Mitchell?), that "She takes just like a woman / She aches just like a woman / She makes love just like a woman / But she breaks just like a little girl." All of us women, living in a man's man's man's world, know only how to break like little girls, to break down like prepubescents, to cry in a manner that is utterly unthreatening, that turns anger to fragility, that preserves relationships just as it destroys our individual integrity. Most of us know how to cry in a way that is no threat to the status quo, in a way that creates a detente over all fights within a relationship (What better way to curtail a vi-

cious, violent row between equals than to have one party begin to cry and evince vulnerability?), and therefore, if the
personal is political, prevents any change in relations between the sexes in larger society.

So I imagine a world—in fact, I dream of a world—in
which tears are a sign of strength, in which the emotion pro-
jected is not just that of a frail wail. Because I am someone
who lived with a severe depression for more than a decade, I
know some version of this universe. For a good ten years—
and during many recurrent bouts since I was finally properly
treated for the disease—I spent a great deal of time crying to
no one in particular about nothing specific, just howling at
the moon, lunatic-ing, as it were. I know the strange power
of a pain so deep no one can reach it, no one can touch you,
every attempt to come close is so exasperating that the sorrow can be strangely compelling to anyone outside of it. As a
chronic depressive who is well acquainted with very black
moods and a creepy sense that an ocean is breaking inside
her brain, I know what it's like to have tears so violent and
extreme and profuse flow from within me that they cannot
possibly have a mitigating effect on anyone nearby. I know
about the kind of tears that frighten the hell out of people, I
know about the tears of a person going insane, tears pro-
pelled by craziness that alienate the whole world with their
scary power. I know about freak-show crying. The only crying I have known to express strength has also been that
which denotes derangement—and hence unfitness for society, and hence weakness.

But the Indigo Girls changed that for me. Melissa
Etheridge, too. Don't know quite why, can't say for sure, but
somehow the often overwrought and emotionally needy
songs they sing are marvelous expressions of strength.
Strength of character, I guess: They are so direct in all their
want, so indelicate in all their desire, so deliberate in all their
demands that the honesty shows a conviction about what
they have the right to need. And by claiming this right, these

expressions of weakness become fighting words. When, in the song "Blood and Fire," in an artlessly pathetic plea by Amy Ray for a lover to come back so she will stop spending nights burning herself with matches and cutting herself up with razor blades, she starts to rant, "I am intense I am in need I am in pain I am in love," the bluntness is over the top. There is no poetry here, there are barely even instruments in the song—just voice and acoustic guitar—and it is precisely this sort of insistent mockery of all traditional musical structures that demand some conformity to meter and verse, rhyme and melody, that gives the song emotional power. Sorrow supersedes artistic considerations in a way that is grating to many, but absolutely liberating to others.

Likewise, Melissa Etheridge has a song called "Like the Way I Do," which is nothing more than a jealous rant in a hard-rock key that asks, in its chorus: "Tell me does she want you, infatuate and haunt you / Does she know just how to shock you, electrify and rock you / Does she inject you, seduce you and affect you like the way I do?" Of course, the only answer to this question, obviously rhetorical in its desperation, has got to be some version of no. Once again, the plea is so over the top, so raw and crazed, so brimming with florid images of *Fatal Attraction* femaleness, that it feels more lethal to the average man than the notion of a black widow spider who kills her lovers after sex. I mean, at least the arachnid gets it over with fast. But the narrator in Melissa Etheridge's song has the makings of a knock-down, drag-out stalker. (In fact, on that same debut album, a cut called "I'll Be Watching You" presents the point of view of a stalking woman—and treats her loitering outside a would-be lover's window as if it were perfectly normal.) When I first heard this song in 1988, I had no idea that Melissa Etheridge was gay, and I thought she gave voice to us obsessive, neurotic women who long to be this direct and obvious about the neediness we feel for the men in our lives.

I should have known, instinctively, that the song could

only have been directed at another woman. "Like the Way I Do" is, as has become clear to me in hindsight, as much a song of liberation as it is a ballad of romantic captivity. Because to yell this loud—and, no less, to do it inside the macho confines of a rock 'n' roll echo chamber—about a love that dares not speak its name is by definition to set your spirit free. Perhaps the joyfulness that I feel seething, overbrimming, from so much lesbian music, even when it is at its most heartbreaking, has to do with the simple fact that just to have the courage to find a voice to sing with in the context of societally censored desires means that anything you say, no matter how depressing the thought, will never ever come across as completely dispirited. To watch Melissa Etheridge perform her overplayed hit "Come to My Window" at the 1995 Grammy Awards, to see her suddenly give that by now tired tune some new guts by pumping a real passion into the lines, "I don't care what they think / I don't care what they say / What do they know about this love anyway?" is to understand that singing about a love forbidden—singing it out anytime anyplace anywhere anyhow—will always be committing an act that is thoroughly and subversively spirited.

And who among us, gay or straight, has never felt a love that is too deep or too strong—for someone too old or too young; for someone married or otherwise unavailable; for someone of a different race, religion, nationality, or political party; for someone who drinks too much, who drugs to oblivion; for someone who beats and maims us; for someone who smashes windows and breaks furniture; for someone who makes us feel too crazy, too obsessed, too nuts, too ready to murder, to leave home, to defy our parents, to rob banks, to set houses on fire, to curse God, to join a cult, to kill our own children, to despise ourselves, to destroy our own flesh? Who has never had a moment of obsessive forbidden love? He among us who is without sin—as a certain martyred messiah might have put it—may cast the first stone at Ms. Etheridge.

. . .

While all of Melissa Etheridge's emotional excess has mostly gotten her branded as uncool, suburban, stonewashed, hokey, the antithesis of the hip, alternative music that all the grunge kids are listening to—in fact, coming out has actually given her, along with a better hairstyle, some new cachet and credibility among the smart set—the Indigo Girls are more likely to be dismissed outright. They are frequently written off as dykey, corny, earthy-crunchy, mushy, irritating, and, most importantly, self-indulgent and painfully emotional. One person I know sees them as the girls who lived down the hall from you in your freshman dorm, the ones who sang "Kumbuya" around the campfire: they are very talented amateurs, white girls with no edge.

But you see, I too am a white girl with no edge. And I feel so stupid about it, so apologetic, so persistently conscious that with all the trouble in the world, all the Bosnias and Rwandas to contend with, my problems seem so silly, so worthless. I feel ridiculous every time I want to scream out, "I am intense I am in need I am in pain I am in love." I feel like an idiot every time I think of the *New York Times,* the UN, the EEC, the former Soviet Union, the search for a cure for breast cancer—all those important macrocosms I wish I could be more engaged with. Instead, my life seems to be about stupid girl stuff. But the Indigo Girls appear utterly unconcerned with this hierarchy of worthy troubles.

Of course, they *do* sing songs about the environment and the like, and maybe that vindicates all their odes to the inner life. But I don't get the feeling that they work out some equation that says every song about Greenpeace can be countered with a couple of tunes about private matters. One of the advantages of being part of a sexual minority in this country is that very strong political movements have been built around what, on a person-by-person basis, amounts to nothing more than who it is that you choose to go to bed with. Sex—or, more specifically, certain sex acts—starts to encompass everything: community, religion, lifestyle, all that matters. So it is that in the Indigo Girls' world, every bit of romance carries with it the weight of thinking globally and acting locally. But this is not a strained or strident quality: their songs have a moral, soulful, even gospel component to them that the Girls seem to come by quite naturally, probably without thinking about it much at all.

And I wish that I, a straight girl, a girl so straight I've never even had a lesbian experience, could know such freedom.

But back to the Greeks, to the time when men had such trouble expressing melancholy in a public forum that they had to hire distaff professionals. In some ways, this skewed division of labor persists thousands of years later in the world of rock music. For women have always been the songbirds of sorrow—Joni Mitchell was simply the best of them—while it has mostly been left in the hands of men to express just about everything else. In recent years many women have crossed gender lines to be tough, like Chrissie Hynde and Patti Smith, or to be blunt, like Liz Phair and Tori Amos, or to be angry, like Polly Harvey and Courtney Love. But everything about these girls who rock is stylized, sexy, brazen, mostly in the way any one of them rubs her crotch on the piano stool or wears kinderwhore baby-doll dresses that pay ironic homage to little-girl Lolitaism with an angry edge. Every one of them functions through that old Madonnaism that insists that liberation means being in control of your own sexuality while ignoring the simple fact that real freedom is being not so terribly concerned with one's sex appeal at all.

Every one of these women—while defying the male rock 'n' roll dictum that says a girl must sit quietly, shut up, and open her mouth only to suck my dick—is still doing it on male terms, still hell-bent, on some level, on showing you, baby, that a woman can be tough. Every minute that these women devote to saying "fuck you" to male standards, they are simultaneously as obsessed as ever with creating a new, hip aesthetic that they hope men will like every bit as much as they used to like big blondes with big tits. Yes, they have made a breakthrough, because their efforts have probably actually changed what men find appealing in women, but despite the change in rules, this is still the same old beauty contest, albeit with much improved standards.

And why should it be otherwise? These women are heterosexual, as am I, and we therefore spend a lot of time worrying about boys, even when we do all sorts of things that are supposed to be telling everybody out there that we don't care about the patriarchy and all that. To be a woman who loves men is, in some way, to never completely get the fuckers out of your head. Martin Luther King once said, "I will not let my oppressor dictate the terms of my resistance," but if Liz Phair's first album, *Exile in Guyville,* is a song-by-song response to the Rolling Stones' *Exile on Main Street,* there should be no doubt about who invented the wheel and who is simply finding new ways to spin it.

Even Courtney Love, whose stage presence is as rough as any chick rocker's, plays it with an air of coquettishness, a quality of flirtation, an ecdysiast's teasing approach to baring all (it's no surprise that she used to be a stripper). And even Chrissie Hynde, the gutsiest woman to come out of the punk rock scene and make it as a certified pop star, had so much style, so much sex appeal, so much leather and tight jeans and thick black eyeliner involved in her presentation. It is all, in the case of every girl singer I can think of, so contrived, so much about the offstage antics and off-putting attitudes that create a crowd-pleasing image that she feels she must convey of what a rock 'n' roll girl ought to be.

What is surprising to anyone listening to the Indigo Girls or seeing them onstage is that they are so natural, so unsneering, so unaffected, so lacking in the kind of self-consciousness that makes it de rigueur in the usual female-rock repertoire to remind us—and remind us and remind us—that anything boys can do, girls can do better. The Indigo Girls don't seem to be concerned with that thought because they are beyond it, outside the purview of the male gaze, beyond the space that is ruled by some imaginary figure like the hierophant card in the tarot deck, the symbol of God the Father, the paean to arbitrary judgment.

Still, there is something condescending and grotesque about—and surely there is some small element of straight-girl superiority in—even contemplating these issues. After all, I'm talking about a bunch of artistic qualities I admire in lesbians, while at the same time absolutely positively reveling in my heterosexuality. Is this not all some peculiar exercise in bestowing my approval—"my" meaning that of any non-lesbian woman—on a poor beleaguered minority? Does all of this not have that vague ring of, say, a nineteenth-century British colonizer's infatuation with the Negro primitives in Africa? Or of the average white American's smug—and, in his mind, generous—assumption that black people have natural rhythm or make better basketball players? Is there not something inherently wrong—even sick—in examining the traits of a historically oppressed group of which I'm not a member, even if the intentions are decent and the ultimate point is to pay homage? What can one make of an essay that appraises and praises the work of women who don't interact sexually with men, written by a woman who is downright boy-crazy? Because all the while that I'm saying such nice things about the Indigo Girls, I'm still really glad to be straight, still would hate to contend with the difficulties that society imposes on gay people, and still would hate to lose the desire—the often painful, confusing, and difficult desire—for that which is absolutely other to me. I would hate to ever give up men. I would hate to be a lesbian. I would just hate it.

Years of feminist indoctrination have done nothing to make me any less male-dependent. That's why, whoever it

was back in the radical seventies—Andrea Dworkin, probably—who declared that you could not be a real feminist and
still be a lover of men was definitely on to something: put
men anywhere in the picture, and they inevitably end up all
over it.

That's why it is, ultimately, "okay" for me to be praising
lesbian art in this manner. Because desire is not a matter of
choice. Who the hell would choose to be enslaved to all the
angst that men bestow upon women? And likewise, who the
hell would choose to put up with all the discrimination and
dyke-bashing you'd have to suffer as a lesbian? It's obvious
to me that whichever way you swing, it has to be an extreme
compulsion. I didn't choose to be straight any more than the
Indigo Girls chose to be gay, and in both cases we are stuck
with the artistic consequences of our God-given, or socially
conditioned—choose your own theory of human develop-
ment—sexual proclivities. I wonder if there isn't some interesting, particularly straight quality in my work that the
Indigo Girls, if forced to undertake this same exercise,
wouldn't find somehow enviable.

The night of the Beacon Theater concert, there was a party
for the Indigo Girls after the show, where I had a chance to
meet them. Each of them emits such a different, distinct aura
that it often seems amazing that they are able to negotiate a
satisfying and successful creative partnership. They don't
write any songs together, and perhaps the fact that they
switch off doing lead and harmony vocals, depending on
who actually penned the tune, allows them the right amount
of elbow room to toil together comfortably. At any rate, how
very different Emily and Amy are becomes particularly apparent when you see them offstage.

Emily, like many of her songs—which occasionally dip
into the realm of John Denver—has a real sweetness about
her, a folksy, earth-mother quality that makes you half expect
to see her walking around in an apron and offering people

freshly baked hash brownies. She's a down-home Georgia
girl by appearance, and the lack of edge in many of her com-
positions makes me think that if she were a solo artist, she
might well get stuck in the lesbian ghetto of itinerant folkies
like Holly Near who never make it in the mainstream. Of
course, Emily has written all of the Indigo Girls' biggest
hits—like "Closer to Fine," "Galileo," and "Least Complicated"—and her songs are often more clever, thoughtful, hu-
morous, and hook-laden than Amy's.

But Amy is raw. She's the rock chick of the pair, the one I
find most compelling, most awash with lust. She's written
what I believe are the Indigo Girls' best—or at least most
startling—songs, the ones like "Tried to Be True," "Land of
Canaan," "Pushing the Needle Too Far," and "Three Hits."
Onstage, Amy can sing a song in a manner that is so crazed
and so out there that you can choose either to accept it as a
thick, lush meadow or to let yourself be frightened by it, as if
it were a menacing prickly cactus. Many people think that
Amy positively butchers Dire Straits' "Romeo and Juliet,"
which was already one of the most heartbreaking love songs
ever recorded, even given Mark Knopfler's snarly voice and
ambient guitar lines. But when Amy does it, she abandons all
attempts at reason and temperance that keep the Dire Straits
version from becoming too sepulchral, too funereal, too dire.
When Amy sings "Romeo and Juliet," she takes the moments
that Knopfler invests with the most irony in his delivery and
overwhelms them with utter, incurable sorrow. I admire her
for feeling so free to be so overwrought, especially since it
comes simultaneously in a package that is very harsh and
cool.

This is something straight girls can't do: they're either hysterical (Sinead O'Connor, Tori Amos) or they're cool
(Chrissie Hynde, Patti Smith), but never both at once. Courtney Love appears to be playing both parts, but I think she's
just a very good actress.

Anyway, I suppose it's clear that if I were going to be attracted to either of the Girls, it would have to be Amy. Funny thing is, that first night I met her, Amy was wearing this black leather motorcycle jacket, these tight jeans and boots, this spiked belt, and she had this very mod shag haircut, and she looked so very pretty and fit and hale in all her butchness that my first thought was, She should have some fabulous boyfriend. She should be with some great-looking guy, some very strong outlaw type, like the Scott Glenn character that Debra Winger runs off with in *Urban Cowboy.* I found myself wanting to fix Amy up with the right man. I wanted to grab her and pull her out of this stupid fern bar filled with granola-girl groupies and take her to a place where she could find the perfect guy, maybe to the Hoboken Motorcycle Club or maybe just to somewhere in Montana. The point is, I wanted her to have a really hot boyfriend.

Was this a displacement of my own lesbian desires? That would be the obvious thing to assume, and I'm willing to consider the possibility. But I actually think it was almost a nonsexual urge. I wanted to be able to sit with Amy and talk about boys, tell her about my boyfriend and hear about hers. I wanted us to be the same. I wanted us to have the same feelings about men, because I wanted to believe that she could be like me and still be as ridiculously cool as she was. Of course, it's just not true. Janis Joplin was as close as it ever got to a man-loving woman who opened herself up so completely and still always seemed so tough, so rough, so able to transmit a message that her vulnerability was part of all this cool.

Then look what happened to her.

But Amy gave me a new idea of how I could be as a woman performer, how I could be controlled and crazed all at once, how I could own that distinctly male rock star quality that allows all the ranting and raving to project itself into desire instead of need, into a catcall and not a caterwaul. I had caught a glimpse of what such an icon-come-to-life would look like earlier in the evening when the Indigo

Girls—with Amy taking the lead—did a high-strung electric cover of "All along the Watchtower," a version that derived much more from Jimi Hendrix than from Bob Dylan. In fact, for a moment, I had forgotten that Hendrix *hadn't* written the song, because they'd played it so loud, so metallically loud, as smashingly noisy as any band of boys, even though they are a folk duo of girls.

And it was somewhere around then, during that particular segment of the concert, that my friend Daphne first pointed out to me that there was something about the Indigo Girls that just kind of had to be lesbian.

Which is why I finally had to concede that it wouldn't be possible for me to ever be anything like Amy. Maybe, just maybe, as a writer, I have managed to have an honesty about myself and my life that borders on brutal, painful, naked, perhaps even, at some moments, alarmingly so. But to write words—flat, two-dimensional, black-on-white words—is not the same as shouting on a mountaintop or singing on a stage. To write words, especially in a multimedia society like ours, often feels about as silent as the proverbial tree falling in the forest. It's easy for me to be as loud as I like in a medium that seems so quiet. To make noise in any form of literature is by definition sexy and sultry, because it gives the page a life, a body, the pungency of a person to hold on to. With good music, those qualities are at the baseline.

So if I had a guitar, if I could sing, maybe I would still be as honest, as raw, as unhinged—but I think I'd be hung up on my own need for prettiness, caught up in my total presentation. I'd still, like Joni Mitchell, end up being a willowy waif, some blonde in the bleachers (in the metaphoric sense, since I am in fact a brunette), some girl singer. Even if I were expressing my most unsanitary and sullied emotions, I'd make them palatable, which is what Joni does so well. There would always be some guy, imaginary or real, whom I would be singing to, and I'd always have to wonder how all this was coming across to him. If I ranted and screamed, if I let out all the ugliness and horror that I feel, would he still like me? Or would all my emotional messiness, all the wallowing, all the aggressive unhappiness, just be a complete turnoff? Would it make me, once again, that thing that I was in high school, that girl no one wanted to take to the prom?

I only ask because it strikes me that growing up, especially if you intend to find an original voice to sing with, write with, or just plain live with, usually involves making a safe break from all the stuff that you always knew was unimportant—even while you let it drive you crazy. It means, in one way or another, leaving the small town for the big city.

When I got to college, I met a lot of other women who had similar versions of this confusion, and all of us have worked it out somehow, so that for the most part we haven't ended up complete sexual deviants. In other words, we got on some socially sanctioned track. But lesbians, with the exception of the small percentage who already knew they were gay and came out in high school, get to have a whole new sexual awakening, a complete rebirth, as they discover their sexual preference sometime in their adult lives. And sexuality is not just about who you're fucking—it's about the life force, the energy source, the complete core of who you are. To experience the transformation of coming out has got to create a break with the past like nothing I will ever know. No matter how many outré things I manage to do with my life, how many body piercings or tattoos or whatever else I might litter my body with, I am still, as a sexual being, the girl my mother wants me to be, the woman who is obedient to the male gaze.

And Amy Ray, I am certain, is not.

If Only I'd Been Born
a Kosher Chicken

by Jyl Lynn Felman

The problem with my mother's dying is not so much that she died but that she died without telling me how to make a chicken. If I could make a chicken the way my mother did, I could have her with me always, or so I imagine. In my fantasy, whenever I want to talk to my mother, I go to the kosher butcher or buy Empire frozen if I'm in a hurry, and I cook that chicken until my mother appears alive and well before me. So strong is the smell of the roasting chicken in my mind that I feel my mother coming into the room this very minute. Before sitting down, without even looking, she automatically reaches toward the table I have set so carefully. She re-arranges the silverware slightly—moving the napkin away from the fork. And then she sits upright and healthy at my own kitchen table. So vivid is the picture that I am smiling, full of our shared presence. As though my mother and I had just spent the afternoon together, talking as we always did. And searching for a way into each other's lives.

Fortunately, both my mother and the roasted kosher

chicken live now in my imagination. But I simply cannot cook. I broil. I grill. I set the table nicely. But I cannot cook at all. Instead, I search everywhere for the perfectly cooked, tender and moist, crisp but not dry roasted chicken. Yet the fantasy is important to me. How could I let my mother die without learning how to cook her chicken? It seems improbable that the thought never occurred to me before she died a year ago. Didn't I know that I would miss her most through the food I eat and the food she cooked? It seems so obvious that I do not know how to cook because I gave up at an early age. I felt for sure that I had to make a choice about my Jewish female future before my future was made for me. Only now, at age forty, my mother gone from me forever by a year, and my Jewish female future made, do I understand how large a mistake I made and how much of the mistake was a product of both my mother's story and my own. For it is in poultry, legs and thighs, breasts and wings, where my mother and I mapped out the fragile borders of our femaleness and made whole the permanent expression of our Jewishness.

My mother washed us both in the same kitchen sink. Only I don't know who came first, the baby or the bird. First I am on the counter watching, then I am in the sink splashing. My mother washes me the way she washes her kosher Shabbas chicken breasts. Slow and methodical, as though praying, she lifts my small right arm; she lifts the wings of the chicken; and scrubs all the way up to where she cannot scrub anymore, to where the wing is attached to the body, the arm to the shoulder. Plucking feathers from the freshly slaughtered bird, she washes in between my fingers; toe by toe. Gently she returns my short stubby arms to the sides of my plump body which remains propped upright in the large kitchen sink. I am unusually silent throughout the duration of this ancient cleansing ritual. Automatically my arms extend outward, eternally and forever reaching for her.

The cold wet chicken, washed and scrubbed, sits next to us on the counter. I weigh more than the chicken, but as far as I'm concerned we're identical, the chicken and I. Except for our heads and the feathers. The chicken has no head and I have no feathers. But I will have hair. Lots of body hair on this nice Jewish girl that my mother will religiously teach to pluck and to shave until my adolescent body resembles a perfectly plucked pale young bird waiting to be cooked to a hot crisp, golden brown and served on the same sacred platter as my mother herself was before me.

At thirteen I stand on the *bimah* waiting to address the entire congregation. I am also upstairs in the bathroom, alone in the terrifying wilderness of my adolescent femaleness. But I stand on the *bimah* and prepare to chant. On my head is a white silk yarmulke held in place by two invisible bobby pins. For the first time in my life, I prepare my female self the exact same way she taught me in her kosher kitchen sink. *Borachu et Adoni hamivorach.* I look out at the congregation of Beit Avraham. My mother is crying. I look in the mirror; I inspect my face, my eyebrows are dark brown and very thick. *Baruch atah Adoni hamivorach laolam voed.* I place the tweezers as close to the skin as possible to catch the root, so the hair won't ever grow back. *Baruch atah Adoni, Elhaynu melach haolam . . .* My parents are holding hands as I recite the third blessing in honor of being called to the Torah. And then I begin. Although my *haftarah* portion is long and difficult I want it to last forever because I love the sonorous sounds of the mystical Hebrew letters. But I am surprised at how much it hurts to pull out a single hair from under my pale young skin. When I reach the closing blessings my voice is strong and full and I do not want to stop.

The rabbi asks my parents to stand. They are kissing me, their youngest baby girl. But I am surprised at how much it hurts to shape my thick Ashkenazi eyebrows into small elegant, anglo female arches. Then I remember the ice cubes that she soaks the chickens in, to keep them fresh and cold before the plucking and how I used to watch her pluck out a long, particularly difficult feather without a single break. She had special *fleishig* tweezers, for use in the kitchen only. The congregation sings, *"Mi chamocha boalim Adoni."* I go to the kitchen for ice cubes wrapped in terry cloth, which I hold diligently up to my adolescent brow. Michamomcha Adoni nadar bakodesh . . . *"Who is like unto thee, O most High revered and praised, doing wonders?"* I have no feeling above my eyes, but the frozen skin is finally ready for plucking.

These first female rituals have no prayers as I stand before the rabbi utterly proud of what I have accomplished. He places his hands above my head. *"Yivorech et Adoni . . ."* He blesses my youthful passage into the adult community of Jews. When I stand alone in the bathroom, my eyes water as I watch the furrowed brow of my beloved ancestors disappear from my face forever. At the exact same moment that I become a bat mitzvah I begin the complex process of preparing myself for rebirth into gentility. I complete these first female rites in silence, without the comfort of my mother or a single Hebrew *brocha*. The congregation rises, and together we say, *"Yiskadel, Viskadesh sh'ma rabo."* Today I am permitted to mourn publicly. I have become a beloved daughter of the covenant, only the covenant is confusing. *Shema Yisrael Adoni echad,* I love my people Israel, but I loathe my female self. Is this what my mother wanted for me? On the occasion of my bat mitzvah my body splits apart and my head becomes severed from the rest of my body, a chicken without a head, a head without a body.

I am balanced precariously between the sink, the toilet, and the cold tile floor. I use my father's shaving cream to hide all traces of the hair growing up and down my legs. I stand with my legs in a wide inverted V and smother my right leg with white foam. My left leg supports my young body while my right leg straddles the sink. Slow and methodical, I scrape the hair off each leg. I have to concentrate very hard so I don't cut myself. Every two minutes I stop to rinse the thick tufts of hair stuck out of the razor. Then I inspect the quality of my work. The finished skin has to be completely smooth, as though there never was any thick brown hair covering my body. Convinced that the right leg is smooth enough, I lower it to the floor. When I am finished shaving my legs, I raise my right arm and stare into the mirror. The hair under my arms is soft, and there isn't very much of it. At thirteen, I do not understand why I have to remove this hair too. As I glide the razor back and forth, I am aware of how tender my skin is and how raw it feels once all the hair is removed. Rinsing off the now clean space, I notice that the skin is turning red. And when I roll on the sticky, sweet-scented deodorant, it burns. But I lower my right arm, lift my left one, and begin again, continuing until I am fully plucked and have become my mother's chicken.

She shows me how to remove all traces of blood from the body. After soaking, there is salting. But the blood of the chicken accumulates under the wings and does not drain out, into her spotless kosher sink. She roasts each chicken for hours, turning the thighs over and over, checking for unclean spots that do not disappear even in the stifling oven heat. With a single stroke of the hand and a silver spoon, she removes a spot of blood from the yolk of an imperfect egg. First she cracks each one separately into a glass bowl; if the yolk is clear, luminous, she adds it to another bowl. But whenever the blood spreads like tiny veins into the center of the bright yellow ball, she throws out the whole egg.

For my turn, I roll the egg slowly in between my palms; I learn to feel the blood pulsating right inside the center so I don't ever have to break it open. I learn that the sight of red blood on the food Jews eat is disgusting. Red juice from an undercooked chicken always makes me gag. I stop eating red meat. I eat all my food well done. I do not tell her when I start to bleed. Instinctively I keep my femaleness to myself. I watch her throw out a dozen eggs, one at a time, crying at the waste. To spill a drop of blood is to waste an entire life.

When I start to bleed, I keep my femaleness to myself. When she finds out, she is furious. How long? I cannot remember. She is hurt. When was the first time? I do not remember. She is almost hysterical, but I cannot remember. I remember only that all signs of blood on the body must be removed. I do not tell my mother when I begin to bleed. Instead I wrap wads of cotton in toilet paper so thick that no one will ever guess what's inside. I clean myself the exact same way she cleans blood from the chickens in her sink. I soak and I salt. I soak and I salt. For hours at a time. For years I will away my own femaleness. I do not spill for months in a row and then, when I do, it's just a spot, a small speck, easily removed like the red spot floating in my mother's yolk.

Before I am born I float in my mother's yolk and I am never hungry. Soon after I am born the hunger begins. By seventeen I am so hungry I do not know what to do with myself. All I can think about is food and how I cannot get enough.

At seventeen I leave the States for Israel. I have to leave. When I arrive *b'eretz* I cannot stop eating. I stuff myself the way my mother stuffs her kosher Shabbas chicken breasts. I stuff myself with grilled lamb shaved right off a hot rotating skewer and stuffed into warm, fresh pita with sauteed onions and lemon juice. In Jerusalem I cannot stop eating as I wait for the bus to take me to the Turkish Bath House where I crouch in the corner on a low stool, sip steaming Turkish coffee, suck on floating orange peels, and stare at all the naked bodies.

I cannot stop eating halvah laced with green pistachios while Mizrachi women with olive skin soak in pools of turquoise water. Slowly, as though praying, they unbraid each other's long, thick dark hair. Standing in water up to their waists, they comb out the knots. They knead their scalps and foreheads gently, washing their hair in the juice of fresh lemons. The women soak in silence. Large round bodies move from pool to sacred pool; hot then cold, tepid, and cool. Back and forth. Tall and thin. Brown skin. Torsos dip and soak in swirls of foaming water. Surrounded by the scent of eucalyptus they soak their feet in burning crystals. Bodies in water float through steam.

I want to take my clothes off, but I cannot stop eating whole figs with date jam spread on fresh Syrian bread while Sephardic women lie on heated marble slabs and close their eyes. Their breasts sag; sunlight doesn't filter in. Bodies in steam float through air. But I am never full. They drink chilled yellow papaya juice from thin paper cups while cooling their sweating foreheads. I want to take my clothes off, but I cannot stop eating. Wings and thighs. Breasts and legs. They soak and they salt in pools of blue water. With avocado soap they wash each other's spines and massage their aching muscles. Jewish women bathe in ancient cleansing waters. Wrapped in soft terry cloth they climb the steps to the roof and begin to eat: plates of hummus lined with purple olives, smooth baba ganhouj and almond macaroons. I can almost touch the sky, sitting on the roof; the Jerusalem sun is hot and strong.

Down below I see the streets of Meah Shearim. Narrow sidewalks and small shops. Women concealed within their bodies. Safely covered from head to toe. Orthodox men in black. Praying as they walk. Their eyes never meet. On the street. Their hands never touch. On the street. Women are covered from head to toe.

On the rooftop women eat, naked in the sun—mothers and daughters, sisters. They lounge on cement slabs, laugh among themselves, and feed each other grape leaves. But I cannot stop eating, staring at the street below. Women with children; live chickens squawking. Preparing for Shabbat. Men in black hats. Long beards. Everything ordered and prearranged. *Ani Adoni Elochechah.* I am the Lord thy God. The Torah is absolute. I love my people Israel. (I loathe my female self.) I cannot stop eating, caught between the roof and the street below. I dream that I am falling, falling to the ground. But I never land. I stay caught forever, hanging limb by limb. Caught forever, limb by limb. The Jerusalem sun is hot and strong. Burning me at seventeen. Suspended as I am. Between my people and myself.

The suspension makes me crazy as I wander the biblical streets. Where do I belong? The suspension is intolerable. I have no place to go. Every week I visit Meah Shearim. Searching not just for my head but for my body too. Every Friday I stay with an Orthodox family and light Shabbas candles as the sun sets. When I'm in my head my body disappears and then I cannot find my Jewish female self. At night I wander back alone from the center of the city to where I live on Har Hatzofim. I search as I walk, staring in the dark, peering into windows, looking for my soul.

In the States, I'm in my body, but I cannot find my head. At home *b'eretz* I eat my way through the city longing to be whole. With my bus fare I buy a kilo of jelly cookies. I eat as I walk in the dark through villages and urban streets. All I do in Israel at seventeen is eat. I tap a hunger so wide that I do not know what to do. I know that I will have to leave the country. There is no one to tell how hungry I have become, because a hunger like this is forbidden.

I have no place to go. I do not know it yet completely. But I fall in love with Israel the way I will fall in love with a woman for the first time. With all my heart and with all my soul. I want to return to the land forever. To live in Meah Shearim. That will save me from my hunger, or so I think and pray. At seventeen I wander the streets of Jerusalem, terrified at what I know I will grow up to be. But there is no one to tell how hungry I have become because a hunger like this is forbidden. I swallow my passion whole; my body swells until I am so enormous that I have to leave the land I love.

Alone, my mother flies to rescue me on an El Al jumbo jet. But I do not say a word. I have become a knaidel, a dumpling, floating in the soup: a nice Jewish girl who doesn't say a word. But stuffed inside my mother's dumpling, swimming just below the surface is a *vilde chaye* waiting to jump out. A wild beast waiting to get out. My mother takes the window seat, staring hard at me, her fat baby girl, drowning in the soup.

As we fly back together, I know that I have failed. She doesn't ask and I cannot tell her what exactly happened. That I fell in love. With Sarah and Hagar, and with Lot's wife the moment she looked back. She doesn't ask and I cannot tell her what exactly happened. That I tapped a hunger I did not know I had. I have watched my mother eat and never gain a pound. She can eat and eat and eat, devour anything in sight, but I never see her body change. I never know what happens to all the food that she consumes. Mine shows on my body, right outside for everyone to see; but the food that she consumes disappears and is impossible to see. My hunger is outside; hers is never seen. Yes, the country's beautiful . . . I did not ever want to leave. And I do not want to cry. Even though I know right inside my mother's dreams for me we can no longer speak.

When we arrive in the States, our covenant begins to break—mother to daughter, daughter to mother. We do not speak the words, but they float between us, growing larger day by day. Right after Pesach, like the first signs of spring, I start to grow all my body hair back again. *A vilde chaye.* She is mortified. It is so soft. She is horrified. I can't believe I ever shaved it off. A wild beast. I run my hands up and down my legs. And when I lift my arms, she turns her head away. She tells me that my body is disgusting. Not a nice Jewish girl, never seen or heard, who does not say a word. I thought my body was my own. More than her knaidel floating in the soup.

The covenant is broken; I've claimed my body as my own. But the silence floats between us, growing larger day by day. What my mother always feared is true. I grow up to be a stunning, raging, wild, forbidden *vilde chaye.* I did not ever want to leave my mother's Shabbas table; but in my twenties, she cannot set a place for me. I learn to close my eyes, light the candles, say the kiddush and the *motzi* by myself. But I cannot cook her chicken so I cannot bring her home to me. And without my mother present, I cannot bear to eat her food.

I become a vegetarian, even though the food tastes strange and never smells the same. With other *vilde chayes,* I make a seder of my own. We become the red beets sprouting green leaves, sitting where the shank bones belong. We wash each other's hands as we pass the bowl around. But we cannot taste our mothers in the soup, and in their absence we grow lame. How can I have my mother and myself? For years we barely speak, and in her absence I grow tame. Only later do I know that her silence is her shame that she gave birth to me, who let my hair grow back. But I did not ever want to choose my mother or myself. And when we, *d'vilde chayes,* call forth our mothers' names: *ematanu, Sarah, Rivkah, Rachel v' Leah,* it is the first time I say my mother's name out loud.

We know that we have been cast out, that our hunger is the shame of both our mothers and our people. Our grief is overwhelming that we have no place to go. Either we are heard among the women but never fully seen or we are seen among our people but never ever heard. There is no language we can speak as we shake our heads in sorrow that we are not counted too.

But I continue to look back, to remember who I am. *Im eshcahac yerushalayim, t'shchah y' menie.* If I forget [Thee O] Jerusalem, may my right hand lose its cunning. I know my mother's waiting and looking back herself. Through her silence she is praying that I will reappear. Through my silence I am praying for my mother to appear. But to reappear is difficult, not knowing what I'll find. At the seder table with other *vilde chayes* my voice grows strong and clear. I learn that I must speak the words to those who do not want to hear. To my mother and my people it's hard to speak what they have always feared. That we are your daughters too and cannot be forgotten or erased.

We are the stories that were never told. We are Shifrah and
Purah, the midwives giving birth. We are Ruth and Naomi
and Boaz's sister Dina. And Sarah and Hagar whom she sent
away. We are Deborah the judge, leading the troops, fighting
on the front. We are Miriam in the bulrushes saving her
brother, Moses. And Rachel and Leah when they were betrayed. We are Vashti who refused and Esther who agreed.
We are all of this and more. This was my mother's fear. That
I was all of this and more. We are the unplucked chickens
squawking in the yard. That the neighbors always see. And at
the weddings and bar mitzvahs we are either not invited or
told to come alone, to be quiet and blend in. But we are your
daughters and cannot be forgotten or erased.

Sometimes we do not look the same; this was my mother's
shame. She did not understand, for as long as she lived, why
I could not look just a little more like her and a lot less like
me. I never understood, until the day she died, why my
mother couldn't be a little more like me and a lot less like
her. My mother too was betrayed. For there was no one she
could tell about her young *vilde chaye* whom she had to love
in secret and never celebrate. The rabbis turned their heads
away and fathers followed suit. The mothers did not talk, or
even whisper by themselves. My mother would not even tell
her younger sister because she was afraid of what the neighbors always say: What will the goyim think? That we are
your daughters. Your sisters and your aunts. And the cousins
in the pictures, standing side by side. *A shunda for d'goyim.*
No one says a word. Instead, they keep the family secret and
only mouth the words. Like how and why and when?

The truth is, I always was just like I am today, only I didn't
know. It wasn't possible as I was growing up to see any other
way. For the longest time I floated in the soup and didn't say
a word. Then one day I had to choose to leap right out of the
bowl. I came to understand that there are those of us who
lead the way and those who like to follow. My mother was a
follower who gave birth to a leader. This was not easy for my

mother or for me. I did not choose to be a leader; it was chosen for me. But what I do not know is if my mother ever felt constrained, as I always did, if it was her choice to follow or if she felt that she had no choice. Perhaps she was afraid to lead—this I'll never know. Yet this is how the cycle flows. In every generation, from follower to leader, *l'dor v dor*. From leader to follower.

All her life my mother didn't understand what it meant to birth a *vilde chaye*. This was my aching disappointment. Before she died, I never had a chance to tell her that to lead, like Moses or Deborah, is to risk the people's wrath. That to be a *vilde chaye* is to live forever on the edge with your life often at stake. I never had the chance to say out loud that I always needed her. My mother's grief at who I am is my deepest sorrow. I wanted her, more than anyone else on earth, to understand and not to be afraid. But this simply wasn't possible; just like me, she didn't know any other way. Sometimes, late at night, when I feel my people's wrath, I wonder, was she right? Is it better not to be seen or heard? A dumpling floating in the soup? Sometimes, late at night, with my life out on the edge, I wonder, was my mother right? Is it better just to be a *bubelah,* a nice Jewish girl, rather than a *vilde chaye?* I always loved my mother and I know that she loved me. The mistake I made is in her chicken that I never learned to cook. From the plucking to the soaking, from the salting to the stuffing to the removal of the blood, we are bound to language and a common history. From the laws of kashruth to the sacred washing of the hands, it is in poultry that we are bound eternal in our femaleness.

In my fantasy I am born a kosher chicken with my mother's hands holding me. She washes me forever in her large kitchen sink. Cleaning my wings, she tells me not to change a thing, that she loves me just the way I am. On Friday afternoons all her Shabbas friends come to see the baby soaking in the sink. They pinch and they poke, laughing at my teeny tiny *polkies.* As a kosher chicken I'd be blessed by the shochet and served on a sacred silver platter with squares of kugel by my side to keep me warm. If only I'd been born a chicken rather than a *vilde chaye,* there would be no painful separation from my mother or my people. I'd be plucked and stuffed, then roasted to a crisp golden brown. Sprinkled with paprika, I'd look gorgeous all the time.

Near the end I washed my mother's hands and feet. She couldn't talk, but she let me in that close. As I washed her legs and thighs, we made a silent, fragile peace; she the perfect *balabosta,* and I, the stunning *vilde chaye.* But in my fantasy I am born a kosher chicken. I sit forever plump and round in the center of my mother's Shabbas table. When she lights the candles and closes her eyes, I am there forever by my mother's side. She is there forever by her daughter's side. We are together, at the Shabbas table, sitting side by side.

The Disappeared

by Jacqueline Woodson

T here is a line . . . thin as thread . . . fragile . . . don't walk, don't step, don't blink or look over there and you're safe. But I've taken a step today and have ended up on this doomed side.

Tick, tock, tick, tock.

There is a clock on the wall behind my friend Renee who sits opening bridal shower present after bridal shower present. She is beautiful in her chair adorned with the colored bows pulled from the gifts, beautiful with pale pastel ribbons strewn around her—so beautiful I forget on this side of the line how much I abhor pastels, how I've learned to wrap gifts with earth-toned paper and twine. My gift to her, wrapped this way, sits waiting to be opened, and now I look at it and realize it's all wrong. I see myself in the mirror that covers the wall behind her in this fancy restaurant and realize that in my navy blue suit with its patterned tie and pin-striped shirt, I'm all wrong amid this crowd of pastel dresses. My locked hair amid the shoulder-length braids and relaxers and pin curls is all wrong. Today, Renee represents what is right. She is dressed in off-white, a dress that curves down to a perfect fit, hair newly relaxed and flawlessly styled, stylish black pumps with stacked heels, perfectly manicured nails—signs of a woman who spends time on herself, not out of vanity but because she genuinely cares how she walks into the world and, unlike me, she has chosen to walk into the world classically, traditionally representing "woman." I have crossed to this side today, and now that I'm here, I am jealous and desirous and . . . goodness, why did I ever lock my hair?

There were four of us then, high school, 1980. Sophia was a year older than the rest of us. At thirteen she had dropped out of Catholic school to give birth to a boy, then Seanie, now Sean. Now Sean is almost grown. He is beautiful and quiet, easy-spirited and too lonely for a teenager. Between his third and fourteenth year, I knew everything there was to know about him. Now we are strangers, states stretching between us like years and water and age and breath.

Sophia was the most beautiful then—bright brown eyes, clear skin, and hair down past her shoulders. She wanted to be a model then, and no one doubted she could be. She could sing any Chaka Khan song flawlessly. If she didn't model, she would sing, and this too we didn't doubt. Cathy was the second most beautiful of us, but she was French and this gave her an edge. When boys flocked around us, she and Sophia would vie for position. If all else failed, Cathy would use her French to woo the few who had, by some strange circumstance, failed to notice her. At fifteen, Renee already knew how to walk the walk that made heads turn, how to flirt and smile and tease. I was tall and thin and pretty but didn't know this. I was careless in my body and my dress. My friends tried to help, and from them I learned with much effort how to act like a lady and, by extension, how to acquire a man. We all had steady boyfriends, nice guys who were basketball and swim team captains, honor roll students and tutors. We sat together at lunch. When Renee ran for class president, I ran for vice president, and we won these races easily. We were cheerleaders and dancers and extremely popular. If anyone had asked, I would have said, yes, we were happy.

Renee pulls a dildo from a box and the women howl. The dildo is bigger than anything I've ever seen. A million suggestions for its use begin to fly, and I sit silent. I am Renee's writer friend, a lesbian who writes books for young people—as contrary as being here trapped between women impatiently waiting for Mr. Right and women who thought they'd found him long ago and now sit complaining over glass after glass of champagne. We are so different, it is almost painful. No. It *is* painful. When I was young, from fifth grade onward, a phrase ran through my head, a line I had read or written or heard whispered somewhere: "We grow up. We grow away." I wondered about the significance of this statement. Once, I thought it meant the distance we place between our parents and ourselves. Now I know it is the distance of childhood and friendships and everything in between.

When she was seventeen, Sophia tried to end her life. She wasn't the only one to die a bit that day. It would take years for us to understand the extent of our grieving, the way each of us grieved for the near-loss of her and our newly emerging comprehension of living.

Renee and I sit at opposite ends of living today—our parallel histories connecting us, a canyon of women dividing us—and I can't help making mental comparisons between her friends and mine. The conversations are different. My friends discuss politics and homophobia in the workplace, the new cute girl at the new queer bookstore, and who's stepping out on whom. Renee's friends discuss men and men and men and marriage and babies, their jobs, and who's stepping out on whom. Men take up little to no space in my friends' conversations. Lesbians warrant the same amount of time in Renee's group of women. Her friends discuss hired help—who can you trust, who knows dirt and how to find it. At the very beginning of this discussion, our worlds—the unsaid ground on which we meet—for the sharpest moment, intersect.

Our grandmothers were domestics, and so were our grandmothers' mothers, and on and on back to a time when there was no pay involved. We are the final generation—our parents' dream children, upper middle class and still upwardly mobile. We drive Volvos and vacation in the Caribbean, we live in brownstones in Fort Greene, Park Slope, Brooklyn Heights. We have bought homes on Long Island, send our children to private schools. And look at our clothes—dresses tailor-made for us or straight out of famous Fifth Avenue stores. We don't skimp.

It seemed inevitable that there would come a moment when Cathy and Sophia came to blows over a man. It happened finally, the summer before we left for college. Siding with Sophia, I lost touch with Cathy, and even now I hear little about her from Renee. That fall we left for four different schools. A year later Sophia would leave school because of financial problems and because her mother could no longer care for Sean.

In college, I pledged Alpha Kappa Alpha, the first black sorority because then, as now, blacks were being excluded. I pledged because I wanted to spend time with black women, wanted a connection. I still believe in that connection, still believe in my sorority, won't let anyone denounce the pledge process, the sorority's colors, or what some deem its exclusivity. In college I came out. Neither pledging nor coming out was easy. Sophia and Renee had a lot of questions but in the end swore they knew before I did. Cathy may or may not have gotten the news. Often I think of her and wonder who she has become. Three years later Sophia married the father of her second child and asked if I'd be her baby's godmother. Her husband vetoed the idea because of my lesbianism. Sophia and I lost touch.

Renee looks over at me and smiles now, dangling the dildo teasingly. It has been only ten years since we were close. And although it is unstated, sexuality is what has come between us. It has informed our choice of community, social life, dress, friends, literature, even restaurants. We are on the outside of each other's lives but hold on to what little is left between us. It is enough, we know. This tiny bit is the call late at night to reminisce. The photo snapped at a book party ("My oldest school friend"), the sincere "How's your mother?" the from-the-gut laugh over some long, long time ago, the soothing words to ease a slight from the vast white world beyond us.

So I sit here, silent on this other side. Silently sipping champagne, silently staring at my hands until Renee's mother says "Jackie has gotten quiet in her old age," and everyone, even the ones who've never known me, laugh, their gazes curious.

In two weeks there will be a wedding. Renee's husband will pull a garter from her leg to the screams and cheers of the audience. Then they will jump a broom in honor of the slaves who didn't have the privilege of lavish public ceremonies. They will receive the best of everything. Parents will beam drunkenly, spoons tapping against glasses to cheer on yet another and another and another kiss. . . .

In three weeks, in a restaurant in SoHo, my lover will lean across our table and say, "Take a chance. Kiss me . . . in front of everyone." And I will, and the woman in the fur coat at the table next to me will scowl, reach across the table, and touch her husband's hand. Later that evening I will dial Renee's number and wait, wait, wait for the last of the familiar calming voices of long ago.

Listening

by Grace Paley

I had just come up from the church basement with an armful of leaflets. Once, maybe only twenty-five, thirty years ago, young women and men bowled in that basement, played Ping-Pong there, drank hot chocolate, and wondered how in God's separating world they could ever get to know each other. Nowadays we mimeograph and collate our political pamphlets among the bowling alleys. I think I'm right when I remember that the leaflets in my arms cried out, "U.S. Honor the Geneva Agreements." (Jack did not believe the United States would ever honor the Geneva Agreements. Well, then, sadness, Southeast Asian sadness, U.S. sadness, all-nation sadness.)

Then I thought: Coffee. Do you remember the Art Foods Deli? The Sudarskys owned it, cooked for us, served us, argued Europe Israel Russia Islam, played chess in the late evening on the table nearest the kitchen, and in order to persuade us all to compassion and righteousness exhumed the terrible town of his youth—Dachau.

With my coffee I order a sandwich named after a neighbor who lives a few blocks away. (All sandwiches are so honored.) I do like the one I asked for—Mary Anne Brewer—but I must say I really prefer Selena and Max Retelof, though it's more expensive. The shrimp is not chopped quite so fine, egg is added, a little sweet red pepper. Selena and Max were just divorced, but their sandwich will probably go on for another few years.

At the table next to mine, a young man leaned forward. He was speaking to an older man. The young man was in uniform, a soldier. I thought, When he leaves or if I leave first, I'll give him a leaflet. I don't want to, but I will. Then I thought, Poor young fellow, God knows what his experience has been; his heart, if it knew, would certainly honor the Geneva Agreements, but it would probably hurt his feelings to hear one more word about how the U.S.A. is wrong again and how he is an innocent instrument of evil. He would take it personally, although we who are mothers and have been sweethearts—all of us know that "soldier" is what a million boys have been forced to be in every single one of a hundred generations.

Uncle Stan, the soldier boy was saying, I got to tell you, we had to have a big wedding then, Mama-san, Papa-san, everybody was there. Then I got rotated. I wrote to her, don't think I didn't. She has a nice little baby girl now. If I go back, I'll surely see her. But, Stan, basically I want to settle down. I already reenlisted once. It would be good if I got to be a construction worker. If you know someone, one of Tommy's friends. If you got a contact. Airfields or harbors—something like that. I could go over for a year or two now and then. She wouldn't want to come back here. Here's the picture, see? She has her old grandma, everybody's smiling, right? I'm not putting her down, but I would like to find a good-looking American girl, someone nice, I mean, and fall in love and settle down, because, you know, I'm twenty-four already.

Uncle Stan said, Twenty-four, huh? Then he asked for the

check. Two coffees, two Helen someone-or-others. While the waitress scribbled, I—bravely, but against my better judgment—passed one of the leaflets to the young man. He stood up. He looked at it. He looked at me. He looked at the wall, sighing. Oh, shit. He crumpled the leaflet in one hand. He looked at me again. He said, Oh, I'm sorry. He put the leaflet on the table. He smoothed it out.

Let's go, said Uncle Stan.

I'd finished my lunch, but Art Foods believes that any eating time is the body's own occasion and must not be hurried. In the booth behind me two men were speaking.

The first man said: I already have one child. I cannot commit suicide until he is at least twenty or twenty-two. That's why when Rosemarie says, Oh, Dave, a child? I have to say, Rosemarie, you deserve one. You do, you're a young woman, but no. My son by Lucy is now twelve years old. Therefore if things do not work out, if life does not show some meaning—*meaning,* by God—if I cannot give up drinking, if I become a terrible drunk and know I have to give it up but cannot, and then need to commit suicide, I think I'd be able to hold out for eight or nine years, but if I had another child I would then have to last twenty years. I cannot. I will not put myself in that position.

The other man said: I too want the opportunity, the freedom to commit suicide when I want to. I too assume that I will want to in ten, twenty years. However, I have responsibilities to the store, the men who work there. I also have my real work to finish. The one serious thing that would make me commit suicide would be my health, which I assume will deteriorate—cancer, heart disease, whatever. I refuse to be bedridden and dependent, and therefore I am sustained in the right to leave this earth when I want to do so and on time.

The men congratulated each other on their unsentimentality, their levelheadedness. They said, almost at the same time, You're right, you're right. I turned to look at them. A little smile just tickled the corners of their lips. I passed one of my leaflets over the back of the booth. Without looking up, they began to read.

Jack and I were at early-morning breakfast when I told him the two little stories. And Jack, I said, one of those men was you.

Well, he said, I know it was me. You don't have to remind me. I saw you looking at us. I saw you listening. You don't have to tell stories to me in which I'm a character, you know. Besides which, all those stories are about men, he said. You know I'm more interested in women. Why don't you tell me stories told by women about women?

Those are too private.

Why don't you tell them to me? he asked sadly.

Well, Jack, you have your own woman stories. You know, your falling-in-love stories, your French-woman-during-the-Korean-War stories, your magnificent-woman stories, your beautiful-new-young-wife stories, your political-comrade-though-extremely-beautiful stories . . .

Silence—the space that follows unkindness in which little truths growl.

Then Jack asked, Faith, have you decided not to have a baby?

No, I've just decided to think about it, but I haven't given it up.

So, with the sweetness of old forgiving friendship, he took my hand. My dear, he said, perhaps you only wish that you were young again. So do I. At the store when young people come in waving youth's unfurled banner "Hope," meaning their pockets are full of someone's credit cards, I think: New toasters! Brand-new curtains! Sofa convertibles! Danish glass!

I hadn't thought of furniture from the discount store called Jack, Son of Jake, as a song of beginnings. But I guess that's what it is—straw for the springtime nest.

Now listen to me, he said. And we began to address each

other slowly and formally, as people often do when serious-
ness impedes ease; some stately dance is required. Listen.
Listen, he said. Our old children are just about grown. Why
do you want a new child? Haven't we agreed often, haven't
we said that it has become noticeable that life is short and
sorrowful? Haven't we said the words "gone" and "where"?
Haven't we sometimes in the last few years used the word
"terrible" and we mean to include in it the word "terror"?
Everyone knows this about life. Though of course some fools
never stop singing its praises.

But they're right, I said in my turn. Yes, and this is in order to encourage the young whom we have, after all, brought
into the world—they must not be abandoned. We must, I
said, continue pointing out simple and worthwhile sights
such as—in the countryside—hills folding into one another
in light green spring or white winter, the sky, which is always
astonishing either in its customary blueness or in the configuration of clouds, the way they're pushed in their softest
parts by the air's breath and change shape and direction and
density. Not to mention our own beloved city crowded with
day and night workers, shoppers, walkers, the subway trains,
which many people fear, but they're so handsomely lined
with pink to dark, dark brown faces, golden tans and yellows
scattered among them. It's very important to emphasize what
is good or beautiful so as not to have a gloomy face when
you meet some youngster who has begun to guess.

Well, Jack said.

Then he said, You know, I like your paragraphs better than
your sentences. That comment wasn't made, I knew, in order
to set the two forms in hostile opposition. It was still part of
the dance, a couple of awkward, critical steps from theory to
practice.

Perhaps, he continued, if we start making love in the
morning, your body will be so impressed and enlivened by
the changes in me that it will begin again all its old hormonal
work of secreting, womb cleaning, and egg making.

I doubt it, I said. Besides, I'm busy, you know. I have an awful lot to do.

By this I meant that our early mornings are usually so full of reading last night's paper, dissenting, and arguing appropriate actions, waking the boys, who should really be old enough to understand an alarm clock when it speaks to them—without their mother's translation. Also, we once had the moral or utilitarian idea that brainy labor must happen early; it must precede the work of love or be damaged by the residual weight of all that damp reality.

But Jack said, Oh, come on. He unbuttoned his shirt. My face is very fond of the gray-brown hairs of his chest. Thanks, I said, but it won't work, you know. Miracles don't happen, and if they do, they're absolutely explainable. He began to get a very rosy look about him, which is a nice thing to happen to a man's face. It's not called blushing. Blushing is an expression of shyness and female excitement at the same time. In men it's observed as an energetic act the blood takes on its determined own.

Think think, talk talk, that's you, stop it! Come on, kid, he said, touching my knee, my thigh, breast, all the outsides of love. So we lay down beside each other to make a child, with the modesty of later-in-life, which has so much history and erotic knowledge but doesn't always use it.

How else is one to extract a new person from all-refusing Zeus and jealous Hera? My God, said Jack, you've never mentioned Greek gods in bed before. No occasion, I said.

Later on he called the store to tell the salesmen not to sell too many kitchen sets without him, he couldn't afford to give away all that commission. Wouldn't you think that would annoy the men? Jack says I don't understand the way men talk to one another.

I had just started the coffee when Richard, my very large and handsome son, appeared. He is known far and wide for his nosy ear. Why are you still in your pajamas? I asked. He answered, What is this crap, Mother, this life is short and terrible. What is this metaphysical shit, what is this disease you intelligentsia are always talking about.

First we said: Intelligentsia! Us? Oh, the way words lie down under decades, then the Union of Restless Diggers out of sheer insomnia pulls them up: daggers for the young, but to us they look like flowers of nostalgia that grew in our mothers' foreign gardens. What *did* my mother say? Darling, you should have come to Town Hall last night, the whole intelligentsia was there. My uncle, strictly: The intelligentsia will never permit it!

So I laughed. But Jack said, Don't you dare talk to your mother like that, Richard! Don't you dare! Ma, Richard said, get his brains out of the pickle jar, it's no insult. Everyone knows the intelligentsia strikes the spark, so that they'll be relevant for a long time, striking sparks here and there.

Of course, he explained, the fire of revolution would only be advanced, contained, and put to productive use by the working class. Let me tell you, Jack, the intelligentsia better realize this. And another thing, where'd you get that don't-dare-talk-to-my-mother stuff? . . . I know her a lot longer than you do. I've been talking to her for maybe almost eighteen years, and you've been sitting around our house maybe three years tops.

Sorry, Richard. I heard a character on a TV show last night say exactly that. "Don't you dare talk to your mother like that." I had gone over to see Anna about something. She turned on the TV the minute I came in.

Wow! Really? Listen, the same thing happened to me too. I went to see Caitlin—you know Caitlin, around the corner, the doctor's daughter. The one whose kid brother tried to set fire to the nun a couple of years ago? Well, you know, she did that too the minute I came in, she turned on the TV.

Huh! They were surprised that the girl and the woman unknown to each other had done exactly the same thing to each of them. Richard offered Jack a cigarette and sat down at the kitchen table. Coffee, Ma, he said.

Then Jack asked, Richard, tell me, do you forgive your father for having run out on you kids years ago?

I don't forgive him and I don't not forgive him. I can't spend my life on personal animosities. The way imperialism's leaning so hard on the Third World the way it does . . .

Jack said, Ah . . . He blinked a couple of times, which a person who can't cry too well often does. Richard, did you know my father was a junk peddler. He had a pushcart. He yelled in Yiddish, "Buy old clothes, buy old clothes." I had to go with him, walk up to the fifth floor, pick up stuff; I guess we crawled up and down every street in the Bronx . . . "Buy old clothes . . . old clothes."

Richard said, Oh!

What do you think? Jack asked. Rich, do you think my daughter, I mean Kimmy, will she ever call me up and say, It's okay, Dad?

Well, said Richard, nodding his head, shrugging his shoulders.

I have to go to work now, I said. I don't happen to own my own business. Also, I have a late meeting tonight. Okay?

The two men nodded. They sat quietly together expanding their lungs to the tiniest thread of tissue with smoke. Breathing deeply, dangerously, in and out.

Then, as often happens in stories, it was several years later. Jack had gone off to Arizona for a year to clear his lungs and sinuses and also to have, hopefully, one last love affair, the kind that's full of terrific longing, ineluctable attraction, and so forth. I don't mean to mock it, but it's only natural to have some kind of reaction. Lots of luck, Jack, I said, but don't come home grouchy. The boys were in different boroughs trying to find the right tune for their lives. They had been men to a couple of women and therefore came for supper only now and then. They were worried for my solitariness and suggested different ways I could wear my hair.

Of course, because of this planet, which is dropping away

from us in poisonous disgust, I'm hardly ever home. The other day, driving down the West Side—Broadway—after a long meeting, I was stopped at a red light. A man in the absolute prime of life crossed the street. For reasons of accumulating loneliness I was stirred by his walk, his barest look at a couple of flirty teenage girls; his nice unimportant clothes seemed to be merely a shelter for the naked male person.

I thought, Oh, man, in the very center of your life, still fitting your skin so nicely, with your arms probably in a soft cotton shirt and the shirt in an old tweed jacket and your cock lying along your thigh in either your right or left pant leg—it's hard to tell which—why have you slipped out of my sentimental and carnal grasp?

He's nice, isn't he? I said to my friend Cassie.

I suppose so, she said, but Faith, what is he, just a bourgeois on his way home.

To everyday life, I said, sighing with a mild homesickness.

To whose everyday life? she said. Goddammit, whose?

She turned to me, which is hard to do when you're strapped and stuffed into a bucket seat. Listen, Faith, why don't you tell my story? You've told everybody's story but mine. I don't even mean my whole story, that's my job. You probably can't. But I mean you've just omitted me from the other stories, and I was there. In the restaurant and the train, right there. Where is Cassie? Where is *my* life? It's been women and men, women and men, fucking, fucking. Goddammit, where the hell is my woman and woman, woman-loving life in all this? And it's not even sensible, because we *are* friends, we work together, you even care about me at least as much as you do about Ruthy and Louise and Ann. You let them in all the time. It's really strange, why have you left me out of everybody's life?

I took a deep breath and turned the car toward the curb. I couldn't drive. We sat there for about twenty minutes. Every now and then I'd say, My God! or Christ Almighty! neither of whom I usually call on, but she was stern and wouldn't speak. Cassie, I finally said, I don't understand it either; it's true, though, I know what you mean. It must feel for you like a great absence of yourself. How could I allow it? But it's not me alone, it's them, too. I waited for her to say something. Oh, but it *is* my fault. Oh, but why did you wait so long? How can you forgive me?

Forgive you? She laughed. But she reached across the clutch. With her hand she turned my face to her so my eyes would look into her eyes. You are my friend, I know that, Faith, but I promise you, I won't forgive you, she said. From now on, I'll watch you like a hawk. I do not forgive you.

Contributors

Dorothy Allison is the author of the novel *Bastard Out of Carolina* (1992, National Book Award Finalist in Fiction); *Skin: Talking About Sex, Class & Literature; Trash* (1989, double Lambda Literary Award winner for Lesbian Fiction and Small Press Book); and *The Women Who Hate Me, Poetry: 1980–1990*.

Gloria Anzaldúa is the co-editor of *This Bridge Called My Back: Writings By Radical Women of Color* (Before Columbus Foundation American Book Award). She is the author of *Borderlands/La Frontera: The New Mestiza, Friends from the Other Side/Amigos del Otro Lado*. She is also the editor of *Making Face, Making Soul/Haciendo Caras*. A popular speaker, teacher, and workshop leader, Gloria is a contributing editor to the journal *Sinister Wisdom*.

Susie Bright is one of the best-known erotic critics and lesbian sex educators in America. She is the author of *Susie Sexpert's Lesbian Sex World* and *Susie Bright's Sexual Reality: A Virtual Sex World Reader.* She edited *Herotica, Herot-*

ica II, and *Best American Erotica, 1993, 1994,* and *1995.* She is the former editor of *On Our Backs* magazine. She lives in San Francisco.

Harriet Brown writes often about issues pertaining to women, children, and families for publications such as the *New York Times, Glamour, Parenting, Health,* and *Healthy Woman.* She has published poetry in *Prairie Schooner* and other literary magazines, and has won numerous awards for her poetry. She lives in Madison, Wisconsin.

Sylvia Brownrigg has written fiction for *Mississippi Review, Event,* the *Louisville Review,* and other publications, and her journalistic work has appeared in the *Village Voice, GCN,* and the London *Guardian.* She is the author of a work of short fiction, *Ten Women Who Shook the World.* She lives in London, where she is at work on a new novel.

Michelle T. Clinton received a 1992 fellowship from the National Endowment for the Arts. She is the author of two books of poetry: *Good Sense and the Faithless* and *High Blood/Pressure.* Her poetry has appeared in *Best American Poetry 1994* and other publications. She lives in Berkeley.

Meg Daly is a poet and fiction writer. She lives in Brooklyn, New York.

Jyl Lynn Felman is the author of *Hot Chicken Wings,* a 1993 Lambda Literary Award Finalist. Her work appears in over twenty-five different journals, anthologies, and magazines, including *Tikkun, The National Women's Studies Journal, Jewish Currents,* and *Bridges.* Ms. Felman is also an attorney who lectures in the United States and England on racism, homophobia, and anti-Semitism. She received her master of fine arts degree from the University of Massachusetts in Amherst, where she was awarded a writing fellowship, and she has taught Women's Studies at Brandeis University.

Jessica Hagedorn, poet, multimedia artist, screenwriter, and novelist, was born and raised in the Philippines and moved to the United States in her teens. Her first novel, *Dogeaters,* was nominated for the 1990 National Book Award. She is also the author of *Danger and Beauty,* a collection of selected poetry and short stories. She lives in New York City, where she is currently working on another novel.

Emily Jenkins is a Ph.D. candidate at Columbia University. Her writing has appeared in *Swing* magazine and *Victorians Institute Journal.* She is at work on a book about the fitness industry and has recently completed a novel for children.

Heather Lewis is the author of *House Rules* (Nan A. Talese/Doubleday, 1994; to be published by High Risk Books in 1995) She lives in New York City, where she teaches fiction at the Writer's Voice. She has just completed a second novel.

Daphne Merkin is the author of *Enchantment.* Her essays and criticism have appeared in a wide range of publications, including the *New Yorker,* the *New York Times, Harper's Bazaar,* and *Mirabella.* She is currently working on her second novel, *The Discovery of Sex,* and is putting together a collection of her essays. She lives in New York City.

Robin Morgan is an award-winning poet, novelist, political theorist, feminist activist, journalist, and editor. She has published fourteen books, including the classic anthologies *Sisterhood Is Powerful* and *Sisterhood Is Global.* A founder and for thirty years leader of the second wave of feminism in the United States, she has also been active in the international women's movement for two decades. She is the international consulting editor for *Ms.* magazine. Robin Morgan lives in New York City.

Lisa Palac is the producer of the erotic virtual audio series *Cyborgasm* and the founding editor of *Future Sex* magazine.

She is currently working on a book about sex and popular culture (Little, Brown). Her work has appeared in *Details,* the *Village Voice,* the *London Observer, Playboy, Penthouse,* the erotic anthologies *Herotica, Herotica II,* and *Best American Erotica 1993* and *1995.* She lives in San Francisco.

Grace Paley's short stories have been published in such magazines as the *New Yorker,* the *Atlantic,* and *Esquire.* She is the author of several collections of short stories, including *Later the Same Day, The Little Disturbances of Man,* and *Enormous Changes at the Last Minute.* She continues to be active in antiwar and feminist causes.

Ann Powers is a senior editor at the *Village Voice.* She has also written for the *New York Times, Rolling Stone, L.A. Weekly, Spin,* and various other publications. She has an M.A. in English from the University of California at Berkeley and is co-editor of the anthology *Rock She Wrote.*

Louise Rafkin is the author of *Queer and Pleasant Danger* and *Streetsmarts: A Personal Safety Guide for Women,* as well as the editor of *Different Daughters: A Book by Mothers of Lesbians* and *Different Mothers: Sons and Daughters of Lesbians Talk About Their Lives* (Lambda Book Award, 1991). She lives in California.

Sapphire is the author of *American Dreams.* Her work has been included in many publications, including *Women on Women, HIGH RISK 2, Critical Condition: Women on the Edge of Violence, Queer City: The Portable Lower East Side,* and *War After War.* She lives in New York City.

Sarah Schulman lives and works in New York City. She is the author of five novels, including *Empathy* and *People in Trouble,* as well as a collection of nonfiction, *My American History: Lesbian and Gay Life During the Reagan/Bush Years.* Her novel *Rat Bohemia* is forthcoming from Dutton.

Bárbara Selfridge has received fellowships from the NEA, the Fine Arts Work Center in Provincetown, and Poets & Writers. Her stories have appeared in anthologies and magazines including the *Caribbean Writer,* the *American Voice, Ploughshares,* and the *Pushcart Prizes 1993.* She has completed a collection of writings entitled *Surrounded by Water.* She lives in Oakland.

Indigo Som's work has been published in various journals, including *Matrix* women's newsmagazine. "The Queer Kitchen" was originally published in *Piece of My Heart: A Lesbian of Colour Anthology.* She lives in Berkeley.

Martha Southgate is a freelance writer who has written for the *New York Times Magazine, Premiere, Glamour,* and other publications. She is also the author of a young adult novel to be published by Delacorte in 1996. Her fiction has been published in *Redbook* and the *Onion River Review.* She lives in Brooklyn.

Lisa Springer, a fiction and essay writer, has been published in *IKON, Cover,* and *California Today.* She grew up in the Middle East and received a B.A. from Barnard College and an M.F.A. from Warren Wilson College. She teaches at NYU and Fordham and is currently at work on a novel.

Gloria Steinem is a founder and now consulting editor of *Ms.* magazine, a founder of *New York* magazine and the Ms. Foundation for Women, and president of Voters for Choice. The author of *Revolution from Within* and *Moving Beyond Words,* she travels extensively as a speaker and organizer.

Sharon Thompson is the author of *Going All the Way: Teenage Girls' Tales of Sex, Romance, and Pregnancy* and co-editor of *Powers of Desire: The Politics of Sexuality.* Her widely anthologized stories and essays have appeared in the *Village Voice, Feminist Studies,* and *Cosmopolitan.* She lives in New York City.

Carla Trujillo, editor of *Chicana Lesbians: The Girls Our*

Mothers Warned Us About, is on the editorial board of the *Lesbian Review of Books.* She lives in Berkeley, where she is an administrator and lecturer at the University of California.

Guinevere Turner co-wrote and starred in the recent film *Go Fish.* She is a graduate of Sarah Lawrence College and lives in New York City, where she is at work on several film and television projects.

Jacqueline Woodson is the author of a number of novels, including *Autobiography of a Family Photo* and *I Hadn't Meant to Tell You This,* which won a Coretta Scott King Award. She is a recipient of the Kenyon Review Award for Literary Excellence in Fiction and has been a fellow at the Fine Arts Work Center in Provincetown and the MacDowell Colony.

Elizabeth Wurtzel is the author of *Prozac Nation: Young and Depressed in America.* She was the popular-music critic for the *New Yorker* and *New York* magazine. Her articles have also appeared in *Mademoiselle, Mirabella, Seventeen,* and the *Oxford American.* Her next book, *Sex as a Weapon,* will be published by *Doubleday* in 1997. She lives in New York City.

Permissions Acknowledgments